Reclaiming Assessment

CHRIS W. GALLAGHER

Reclaiming Assessment

A Better Alternative to the Accountability Agenda

Foreword by **DEBORAH MEIER**

HEINEMANN
Portsmouth, NH

Heinemann
A division of Reed Elsevier Inc.
361 Hanover Street
Portsmouth, NH 03801–3912
www.heinemann.com

Offices and agents throughout the world

Library of Congress Cataloging-in-Publication Data
Gallagher, Chris W.
    Reclaiming assessment : a better alternative to the accountability agenda / Chris W. Gallagher.
        p. cm.
    Includes bibliographical references and index.
    ISBN–13: 978-0-325-00918-6 (pbk. : alk. paper)
    ISBN–10: 0-325-00918-X
    1. Educational evaluation—United States.   2. Educational accountability—United States.   I. Title.
LB2822.75.G35 2007
379.1'58—dc22   2006030207

Editor: Jim Strickland
Production: Lynne Costa
Cover design: Night & Day Design
Typesetter: Gina Poirier Design
Manufacturing: Steve Bernier

Printed in the United States of America on acid-free paper
11   10   09   08   VP   2   3   4   5

To Cady and Erin

Peace and passion, always

Contents

Foreword

Lately I've been struck by the flood of messages in the daily news reminding us that we've missed the boat in trying to reform schools on the failed model of business accountability—whether on a micro level (the shop floor) or on a macro level (where all the bookkeeping scandals are daily exposed). The news, in short, is discouraging.

We are sacrificing engagement, "the heart and soul of education," says Chris Gallagher in this remarkable and important book, *Reclaiming Assessment*. The loss of engagement probably isn't good for the workplace, and it's fatal for political democracy.

"Workers want to be fully engaged" and business "needs a system more compatible with democratic rule," Traci Fenton tells us in the *Christian Science Monitor* ("Democracy in the Workplace," August 23, 2006). Could the current mania for standardization, supported by all the business roundtables and corporate leaders, be just a short-term fad?

Nebraska is betting it is. Teachers, with the support of the state of Nebraska, have taken the idea of accountability and turned it on its head. They have argued that democracy and high standards are tied together, and both require just what Traci Fenton argues for: full engagement and opportunities to "express" oneself "while making a contribution that matters."

Maybe our schools—if given a chance—could even teach business a thing or two about accountability. But it won't happen unless we concern ourselves with what we mean by being *well educated*. It's what we've ignored for years. It's that which lies at the heart of the work Nebraska has undertaken by slowly and systematically insisting that each and every community take responsibility for developing its own definition as well as the ways in which to measure it.

What leads us to keep kids in this artificial environment for so many of their most lively and curious years at an enormous public cost? It had better be important and compelling to citizens and kids alike. But until we challenge each and every community to start thinking about this, it's hard to see how we can expect kids to take their education seriously—as something more than a hurdle we've placed in their path. Because, whatever we think their purpose might be, schools do have an impact. Becoming a good worker—for both the political and the economic health of the nation—can't wait until kids leave school to take hold. If we leave the definition of *good worker* blank, we are endangering the work to be done. Much of our future as a nation is being decided by what happens to children between birth and age eighteen. Teaching our children to become adults is what schools are all about, and a citizenry and workforce trained for fourteen or more years to be passive and bored won't be easily turned around. Yet there is no observer of our schools for the past half century who'd deny that schooling in America is just that: boor-ring and passive. We forget that the idea of spending all of one's preadult life learning to be an adult via formal schooling is a very recent innovation, and an odd one at that. For most of the history of our species, one learned to be an adult in and among the adult community one was preparing to join, engaged at various levels in the real tasks of adulthood. Becoming a grown-up, for good or ill, was learned by observing and joining with grown-ups.

Our schools are not organized for such engagement between kids and adults. Most kids are, as a result, engaged only during the two to four minutes between classes, at lunch and recess time, and whenever they can sneak it in without being caught—like trips to the bathroom. And their engagement is almost exclusively with their own peer world and the huge adult industry that has developed to cater to such peer groups, to turn them into insatiable consumers and, in the process, "teach" them, shape their thinking and tastes.

Yes, the impatient reformers are right that the current system is a hard system to change, but it's unclear whether the supposed reformers really want to change it or just make it tighter and more rigid. The evidence is for the latter. President Reagan's Commission for Excellence in Education initiated the modern wave of reform in 1983 with a rather astounding claim, one that Gallagher notes early on: "If an unfriendly foreign power had attempted to impose on America the mediocre educational performance that exists today, we might well have viewed it as an act of war." Unfortunately, this mediocrity continues to be the case, but it is now mandated under the auspices of precisely those who made this alarmist claim.

It's no accident that virtually no teachers were members of that commission (save one, allows Chris). Thus the commission lost sight of the fact that "teachers are the means, the relationship with students is the vehicle, and professional judgment is the tool" of higher standards, as Chris notes. And thus the inexorable detour we have taken, the wasted time and resources, has led us into No Child Left Behind's insane implementation. The driving force of the NCLB reform is the belief that parents and teachers are the "unfriendly foreign power" and that the expertise belongs to unelected leaders removed from the scene who promise education's salvation.

The dramatic shift from local to centralized expert federal control has not occurred without resistance. We are, among other things, not a passive species at heart, and our political system is still sufficiently intact and robust to not roll over easily. Even if we teachers and parents have been attacked by friend and foe alike for resisting reform, we forget at our peril that our capacity for resisting is our true salvation. So, teachers and parents still resist new ideas. Collaboration must be voluntary and purposive to be powerful, not just an act of going along or getting along or saving one's job. We can urge kids and parents (and teachers) to be better citizens, more compliant, but if their citizenship consists of the right to vote only yes, it may turn out that the imposed reforms are as easily swept away as the reforms of the once mighty USSR.

Reclaiming Assessment was written to tell the story of a whole state that resisted going along with policies that undermined the very strengths of its educational system and the very basic premise of its local political ideal—that "we the people" know best. Of course, we the people don't always agree with me, and at present most Nebraskans haven't strayed very far from their traditional ways in either schooling or accounting. We're not natural revolutionaries, and changes take time to root and cannot be force-fed. We learn best by persuasion and good example—which is what good education itself is all about. And it's what the author of this book forces us to consider above all by his clear and lively grasp of the daily details of how it might work if we took it seriously—as seriously as Nebraska has.

Our leaders can put out reams of pages touting miraculous results built on changes imposed overnight, tales of kids and teachers overcoming all the odds under the influence of high-stakes tests and well-funded innovations, and have still changed absolutely nothing for real. There's a test rise here and a drop there. Five or ten years later, nothing remains—except resistance for the next wave of imposed reform. And all too often the statistical mumbo jumbo regarding both past failure and current success consists merely of artifacts of ingenious statisticians. Humans can be ornery and pigheaded. But if we undermine their power to control their own destiny, what we're left with is a society that cannot teach its young about the value of good ideas, much less anything about the power of democracy. A well-educated public might best be judged by its capacity to distinguish real from phony statistics.

"If we want our children to become empowered adults, who use their minds well, who can stand behind their own ideas, while simultaneously being willing to listen and be influenced by the ideas of others, they must be surrounded by adults who engage in and model such behavior" (Nicholas Meier, 2005, AERA), and who most importantly do so day in and day out—in the presence of the young.

Means and ends sometimes fit well together, and if Nebraska can survive the pressures, it may indeed lead the way . . . over time. In the meantime, we all can learn a lot from its efforts, its steady and modest and honest exploration of how best to hold ourselves accountable for our ideas and our practices. Chris Gallagher has brilliantly laid out the story for us; now it's up to us to act on it.

—*Deborah Meier*

Acknowledgments

Of all the smart, pithy things that have been said about writing, none is smarter or pithier than the gem my friend Steve North offers up: "Learning to write is hard, and it takes a long time." Indeed. But writers who listen—and I hope I am learning, finally, to be such a writer—are never alone. If they listen with just the right mix of humility and courage, they join a chorus of voices, rising as one. Among those who have humbled me just enough to listen and emboldened me just enough to sing are the following:

The Nebraska educators who were kind enough to share their (scant) time and (abundant) insight with our Comprehensive Evaluation Project researchers.

The Nebraska educators who contributed their own wonderful work to this book: Edward Montgomery, Suzanne Ratzlaff, Laura Miller, Teresa Frields, and Julie Dutton (special thanks as well to administrators par excellence Keith Rohwer and Jef Johnston).

The Nebraska educators at the Nebraska Department of Education, especially Doug Christensen and Pat Roschewski, courageous defenders of the democratic faith and the right to learn for all children.

The Comprehensive Evaluation Project researchers and assistants, especially the eminently capable Susan Wilson.

Monty Neill, fighter of the good fight.

Lois Bridges, who initially acquired this project and helped me believe in its potential.

Gloria Pipkin, hands down the best editor I have ever known—my friend, my comrade, my muse.

Jim Strickland, who stepped in at the last minute but brought with him the hard-earned wisdom of a longtime fellow traveler.

Several wonderful administrators at the University of Nebraska-Lincoln (UNL) who have supported me in what is for an English professor an unlikely and perhaps odd endeavor: Stephen Hilliard, Linda Pratt, Joy Ritchie, and Dick Hoffmann.

The readers of various drafts of this book, who have offered thoughtful and generous response: Shari Stenberg, Molly Gallagher,

Erica Rogers, Eric Turley, Heinemann's anonymous reviewers, and the members of UNL's Composition Colloquium.

And of course the most beautiful voices in the chorus that is my life, those who have taught me what it means to listen: Molly, Cady, and Erin.

Recently, Cady made a solemn pronouncement: "Dad, you can't sing." Maybe so. But defiantly—and really, what better way is there?— I sing the praises of all those mentioned here (including you, Cady G.), with the hope that my voice, however thin, conveys something of the warm gratitude I feel toward them.

The writing of this book was supported by a Faculty Development Leave from the University of Nebraska-Lincoln.

Introduction
Reforming Reform

Curriculum Night, Cady's Middle School

Ms. L. is offering her well-rehearsed spiel on the sixth-grade curriculum. She has fifteen minutes before the bell rings and we parents are herded off to another room for another teacher presentation. (Is it science or math at 7:35? We'll need to consult our schedule before we leave this room; the passing period is only five minutes.) I'm struggling to keep up, but some of it sounds good: discussion circles, response journals, research projects. Some of it, though, sounds decidedly less good: cursive worksheets, vocabulary lists, multiple-choice spelling tests.

Ms. L. is more efficient than some of her peers, who—so far—have left time after their presentations for only the briefest of questions, if any at all. (*What can we do to help them with homework? Just stay on them. Should they be bringing home their books every night? Not if they don't have homework from the book.*) I shoot my hand up. I think I hear Molly take a deep breath. (Perhaps she is wondering how successfully I will be able to translate our real questions—*Why the hell is our sixth grader doing cursive worksheets for homework every night? What's with the multiple-choice spelling tests?*—into polite fare.)

"First of all," I say, "I like a lot of what I've heard tonight and I appreciate your time. But we"—and here, with a back-and-forth hand gesture, I generously implicate Molly—"have a couple concerns about the kind of work Cady's being asked to do."

Ms. L. nods, smiles, invites me to continue. "You can ask me about anything," she offers cheerfully.

I continue. "OK. Specifically, we're wondering about the purpose of the cursive worksheets and the multiple-choice spelling tests. It seems strange that they're doing those things in sixth grade."

Ms. L., unflappable: "OK, the cursive writing is a district expectation. That's just for review and we're almost done. They just finished R. The spelling tests are to prepare the kids for the tests they'll have to take. They'll need to know that format to do well on tests."

Still smiling, she asks, "Does that answer your question?"

Defeated, I admit that it does.

Parent-Teacher Conference, Erin's Kindergarten

Ms. H. is telling us a story about how Erin and her friends formed the Nature Club in the new playground. In the hands of a less skilled observer of children, it would be a typical, if charming, story about kids scheming and dreaming. In Ms. H.'s hands, it becomes a story that teaches: the way the children chose the perfect location shows their growing awareness of spatial relationships; the way they worked out the rules for membership shows their increasing sophistication in social relationships; the way they dug tunnels in the piles of wood chips shows how they are developing initiative and using language to work together.

Stories that teach are the stock-in-trade of Ms. H. and her colleagues. As parents, we have seen it again and again: through gentle questioning, the teacher leads the child to tell what she already knows but doesn't *know* she knows. (*How are these two leaves different? What can you tell me about their shape?*) The teacher builds on the child's ideas, slyly adding new information, new ways to think about the problem or question at hand, and the child quickly incorporates these into her own inquiry. (*Yes, well done: those are called veins. See how they form different patterns? Does that make you think that they come from the same kind of tree or different kinds?*) The child walks away with a new understanding but also faith in herself: She knows a lot. She will share what she knows with the other children. (*See? These are veins—like the veins in your hand.*) The teacher, meanwhile, walks away with a new understanding of how the child's mind and heart work. This understanding will become a story that teaches for her colleagues. (*Listen to what this child said; here is what I am coming to understand about her.*) Ms. H. and her colleagues spend more time with each other than other teachers we've known. And it shows: they teach each other how to tell and how to listen to stories that teach.

Her eyes shining, Ms. H. turns our attention to Erin's portfolio: a three-ring binder in which Erin and Ms. H. have collected a variety of artifacts that display Erin's learning. First, a series of photographs. Erin and friends arriving at school, posing in front of their wood-chip tunnel, designing their nature club. Each picture becomes an occasion for a detailed description of how the children learn to work together, how they use their imaginations, how they solve problems.

Next, a set of observations, written by Ms. H. An example:

Observation	Key Experience(s)
11-9—Erin and Ashley presented flannel board stories to the rest of the group after they finished lunch. Some children were still eating, so one child suggested that they were at a "dinner theater." The two stories presented were (1) Goldilocks and the Three Bears and (2) Dinosaur Land.	Initiative Social Relations Language Creative Representation

Each observation records a mere moment: the kids choreographing a dance, building houses and towers with stacking bricks, jumping rope during gym time, taking pride in each other's accomplishments, designing games, and so on. But each moment, perceived by an educator who knows how to watch children, becomes a "key experience."

Finally, a sampling of Erin's artwork. Sketches of playground structures. A monarch butterfly. A series of self-portraits: Erin in tall prairie grass, Erin in a wheat field ("My hair is golden like wheat and it's blending in"), Erin in her Halloween costume, Erin at her grandparents' house for Christmas. Characters from books she's read. Diagrams of classrooms. A menagerie: a bunny, a weasel eating a mouse, a squirrel, a beaver. Her family on a tram in the St. Louis Gateway Arch. And there's writing as well: the alphabet, numbers up to one hundred (more or less), several word families (an, can, pan, dan, man), other random words she knows (mom, dad, go, on, off, pop, Erin, Cady). And again, each image, each word, inspires Ms. H. to offer another story, further insight. "Notice," she says, "how much more detailed her self-portraits have become in the last couple months." "And see," she says, "how she's experimenting with scale with these two drawings, one large and one small."

By the time Ms. H. closes the portfolio, she has revealed for us an Erin whom we recognize but could not have described ourselves. Somehow, she has brought us closer to our own child. And that is her goal. ("Ask her about this," she says; "Have her tell you about the time...")

Ms. H. uses our time together to deepen her own understanding of Erin as well. "Is she like this at home?" she asks. "When she is in this situation, does she usually respond by...?" We do our best to respond in kind: to tell Ms. H. stories that will help reveal an even more complex Erin than the one she knows. We are less competent observers of children than Ms. H., but we share with her a keen interest in Erin's growth.

The conference is only twenty minutes long—just a moment, really. But for us, as parents, it is a key experience.

————————

On Listening (to) Teachers

This book is the result of years of research in public schools, years of reading and thinking about school reform, years of writing and rewriting. But I choose to begin with two intimate moments from my life as a parent because they help keep me grounded. They help me remember what is important about schools, what is at stake in schooling.

For the past several years, it has been my job to listen to teachers—hundreds of them. And when I listen to them talk about their work, I think often of my daughters' teachers. For example, when I hear teachers describe how their lives are defined by the mandates of others—the laws, statutes, contracts, policies, provisions, rules, guidelines, checklists, rubrics, matrices, grids, charts, and graphs that regulate their relationships with kids—I think of Ms. L.

At the time, I must confess, I was merely frustrated by what I took to be Ms. L.'s evasion of my serious parental concern about my daughter's education. But over time, I have come to see that a variety of forces conspired to shut down the conversation we could have had with Ms. L. In fact, Ms. L. was doing her job, precisely as she and her superiors understood it. And despite my brief and ineffectual challenge to the script, we parents, too, dutifully played our appointed roles. Ms. L.'s task on curriculum night was to provide *accountability*, in the form of a rational, efficient, and clear explanation of our daughter's curriculum—an account. In turn, our job was to take in the information, maybe offer up a clarifying question or two, and move on. We weren't supposed to talk *with* Ms. L.; we were supposed to be talked *to* by her. Account-ability is a one-way street.

More disturbing yet, this one-way street is paved by the unquestioned authority of effectively anonymous folks remote from the scene of teaching and learning: in this case, district administrators and test makers (though we could certainly add state and federal policymakers, school "reformers," textbook companies, and a host of others). Everything about that night at the middle school—from the inflexible, ridiculously tight schedule to the canned spiels to Ms. L.'s party-line answers—taught us what the kids and the teachers in this school already knew: *they* control things around here; we do not.

I am haunted by the conversation I did not have with Ms. L. In the end, though, it's not my defeated silence I want most to overcome, but hers. The saddest part of this whole affair for me is that we never did hear Ms. L.'s voice. I have a strong suspicion that much of the time, Ms. L. feels much like I did that night: talked to, but not listened to.

But sometimes, I *do* hear teachers' voices, and when this happens, I find myself moved by their careful observations of children, their rich descriptions of teaching and learning, their insightful conversations— their stories that teach. At these times, I think of Ms. H. and her colleagues and how they invite others—children, each other, and parents—into meaningful conversations. They understand the importance of partnerships, of working together to support students' growth. They don't merely do the bidding of remote experts; they put children's learning where it belongs: in the hands of the children and those closest to them, parents and teachers. In doing so, they go well beyond providing an *account* of their curriculum; they *engage* kids and their various educational partners.

Engagement, these teachers have taught me, starts with listening. Teachers are their best teaching selves when they are listening to their students. Although we tend to think of listening as passive, merely receptive, serious listening entails responsibility and reciprocity. It requires diligence, discipline, and a willingness to think from perspectives other than our own. It is hard work. It is the work of teaching, this business of taking other people seriously.

In turn, listening to *teachers*, taking them seriously, ought to be the work of anyone who thinks she has something important to say about education. If this book has anything of value to contribute to teachers' work or to their understanding of that work, it is because every idea, suggestion, and example in the book is drawn from the work of actual teachers in actual classrooms and schools.

The research that informs this book was conducted in the state of Nebraska under the auspices of the Comprehensive Evaluation Project (CEP), a university-based evaluation of Nebraska's standards, assessment, and accountability system (more about this system in a moment). I have served as coordinator of the CEP since 2001. Since that time, we have interviewed more than five hundred and surveyed approximately four thousand Nebraska teachers, administrators, and local school board members. We also have observed dozens of meetings, workshops, and inservices around the state and contracted with educational researchers to conduct statistical studies. (For a more thorough overview of the CEP, see Chapter 3.) But our most important task was to gather voices from the field: to understand what was happening in Nebraska schools from the perspectives of teachers. This book, then, is my best effort to make sense of what my colleagues and I hear when we listen to teachers.

Getting the Wrong Idea

Few so-called reformers are listening to teachers these days. Instead, they treat teachers as executors of the designs of remote "experts": policymakers, administrators, politicians, university researchers, test makers, textbook companies. As a result, teachers spend their days rendering unto Caesar rather than tending to their students. They are made to feed the system because the system, goodness knows, must be fed.

And yet, teachers remain the target of reformers' self-serving agendas: the problem, not the solution, to what ails the schools. The "education establishment," we are told, cannot reform itself; it must be reformed from the outside. No need to listen to teachers; all we will hear are excuses and whining.

This kind of antiteacher thinking buttresses school reform as a remote-control activity. Although educational history is littered with failed programs that imagined school reform as a *technical problem*, not a *people problem*,[1] reformers stubbornly insist that the way to reform schools is to "design controls," as Linda Darling-Hammond puts it, rather than "develop capacity" (1997, 6). Nowhere is this clearer than in the astounding vigor with which proponents of high-stakes testing pursue their Holy Grail–like quest for the Perfect Test. Surely, they seem to think, if we could just get the specs right . . .

The principal argument of this book is that the current accountability-through-high-stakes-testing approach to school reform is all wrong. In an era defined by the sweeping No Child Left Behind (NCLB) Act of 2001 and the implementation of high-stakes state testing in almost every state,[2] this claim might sound heretical, or at least childishly obstinate. Who actually *wants* to leave children behind? Who refuses to see that testing, as President Bush has intoned on more than one occasion, is "the cornerstone of education reform"?[3] But we forget that these "commonsense" questions emerge from a particular perspective, a peculiar logic—an agenda. And it's an agenda, I will argue, that is doing grave damage to our schools and our democratic republic.

Accountability logic is rather simple—and familiar: Schools must prove to those who pay the bills—taxpayers as well as parents, who invest human capital—that they are a good investment. And they must do so by performing well in a competitive market. They must show *results*, expressed in terms of achievement scores (account-ants need numbers). If they underperform, they must adopt the practices of higher performers (i.e., standardize). Complacent or incompetent workers (teachers) must be retooled or let go. Efficiency and economy must be paramount. All of these demands are leveraged by the imposition of incentives and disincentives. A stern hand is needed; direction must come from the top. Compliance equals success; just do as you are told.

Although this business model is often presented by its adherents as good old-fashioned American common sense, a number of critics have emerged to question its application to public schooling. School reform researchers are skeptical of the claims made for top-down, compliance-based school reform. Recent studies show that states with high-stakes tests are *not* seeing the kinds of student achievement gains promised by proponents of the accountability agenda. Instead, those testing regimes are spawning a wide array of unintended negative consequences, including mishandlings and misuses of test data; severely narrowed or watered-down curricula; a sense of impotence and alienation among teachers; student apathy and disengagement; public mistrust; emphasis on raising test scores even at the expense of meaningful learning; kids dropping out or being pushed out at key testing moments; and more. Perhaps most disturbingly, high-stakes testing is making it all the more likely that the students who most need rich, engaging instruction— particularly kids living in poverty and racial minorities—will in fact get little more than intensive test prep. However noble the rhetoric of No Child Left Behind might seem, it is proving to be a disaster for kids'— and teachers'—civil rights.

Meanwhile, state legislatures (Utah's and Virginia's, for instance), teachers' unions, and advocacy organizations such as FairTest have opposed the law. Parent and student activist networks (such as Cambridge Parents Against MCAS and Students Against Testing) have sprung up around the country to oppose the way in which standardized testing systematically discriminates against certain groups of students. Educators have stepped forward to testify that top-down standards, assessment, and accountability systems undermine their professionalism and create school environments that prize winning over learning. Even the psychometric community, which has much to gain by the current high-stakes testing craze, has warned about the severe limitations and unintended consequences of standardized tests, especially when high stakes are attached.

In short, lots of people think NCLB and its emphasis on high-stakes testing are a bad idea. But few observers have challenged the idea of accountability itself. Most seem hopeful of finding new and improved methods of holding schools accountable. My argument goes deeper: Accountability itself is a bad idea. It is a one-way responsibility model premised on *trans*actions rather than *interac*tions. It is about getting what you pay for and paying for what you get. Certainly, there is a *kind* of mutuality here, but it is severely constrained—as it is in all commercial transactions—by bottom-line self-interest. One's participation in transactions is motivated by what one owes or is not owed—not by a shared commitment to a valuable cooperative effort. This approach might serve us well in many areas of life: shopping or dining at restaurants, for instance. But it will not do in public schooling, where we are dealing not with the manufacturing, buying, or selling of commodities, but with the care and keeping of human beings.

We need a better idea.

Getting a Clue

Picture the following newspaper headline: "The accountability movement is dead." The subheading might go something like this: "Teachers and students reclaim public education, usher in new era of school 'reform.'"

Hard to imagine? Maybe so. This kind of momentous shift in the way we think about school reform is unlikely to happen all at once. But as I suggested earlier, the shift has begun. The voices of protest grow ever louder and the hunger for a better way grows more intense. At the risk of sounding faux prophetic, I submit that the next generation of school reform is on its way.

What will this twenty-first-century approach look like? For the most part, we can only guess. My hunch—and my hope—is that the new model will turn the old one inside out. It will dismiss accountability as its guiding principle and adopt instead the more robust concept of *engagement*. Its aim will be to nurture mutually responsible partnerships that are not reducible to bottom-line transactions (a compliance approach), but are instead marked by rich and dialogic interactions (a commitment approach). It will return teaching and learning to teachers and students. It will give teachers the tools and the trust they need to practice their art. It will put the public back in public schools by emphasizing the building of democratic relationships. Indeed, it will make democracy both the *means* of learning (what teachers and students do) and the *object* of learning (what teachers and students learn about). It will create schools that honor the fundamental democratic principle that people ought to have a say in the decisions that affect their lives. It will take seriously the notion that schools are not competitive organizations but rather, as Paul Theobald says, agents for the restoration of community (1997, 2).

As my imagined newspaper subheading suggests, teachers and students will lead the way because it is on their interaction that the whole enterprise of schooling hinges. If schools are where young people learn democracy—where they learn to be democratic citizens—then their relationships with their teachers and peers are paramount. These relationships must be built around a shared commitment to teaching and learning, not on compliance to laws and policies promulgated by remote, effectively anonymous others.

But teachers and students alone cannot fashion engaging schools. A school cut off from the community in which it operates cannot be an engaging school. As Ms. H. taught us, educating Erin (or Johnny or Susie . . .) requires a network of support inside and outside the school. Schools can function as "workshops of democracy" as Gerald Bracey (2002, 104) (after Benjamin Barber) calls them, only if they are of the people, by the people, and for the people.

Fortunately, a number of networks and organizations devoted to creating engaging schools and school systems have emerged in recent years. These include the Coalition of Essential Schools, the National Coalition of Education Activists, the National Network for Educational Renewal, FairTest, and others. These networks and organizations provide useful resources and heartening examples of teachers, students, and communities working together to improve schools. But at the same time, we are seeing very little such work at the *state* level, where the dominant posture is resigned compliance. Those doing the good work of these organizations and alliances find themselves swimming against the stiff tide of top-down state requirements designed to do the bidding of an even more top-down federal government.

If we are to realize a twenty-first-century approach to school reform, we will need to return to John Dewey's fundamental principle of democratic education: that we must provide for *all* children the quality of education the "best and wisest" parent wants for her child ([1900] 1956, 3). In a democratic society, engaging education is not the privilege of the few; it is the right of all. This does not mean—as it does under accountability regimes—that one size fits all; what Dewey was talking about could not be further from standardized, high-stakes testing regimes. Instead, he saw the need to create systems in which knowledgeable professionals practiced their art adaptively and students learned in ways that honored their individual and social-group differences.

Charting by Nebraska's STARS

Maybe this engagement idea sounds pie-in-the-sky. Wishful thinking. A dream. But I'll demonstrate in Chapters 2 and 3 that engagement is a much more reasonable and appropriate approach to school reform than is accountability. Accountability is neither natural nor inevitable. In fact, embedded in it is a worldview that runs counter to the mission and nature of public education.

But as much as I might wish that engagement were such a profoundly and self-evidently good idea that teachers, policymakers, and everyone else would drop this harmful fascination with accountability, I know that's not going to happen. The history of school reform is full of good ideas (and not a few bad ones) that could not stand the test of practice. Some were impractical; some generated unforeseen consequences; some couldn't enlist the support of those who matter most in education: teachers and students.

It won't do, then, simply to declare ideas essentially good or bad; the test of the value of ideas is their fruit, their consequences. We must examine what they *do* and what they *render*. We must ask: What does this idea make possible and what does it make impossible? How does it help us ameliorate or at least cope with important problems? What new problems does it generate?[4]

In Chapter 2, I explore what accountability does and renders. The picture, as I've already suggested, is not pretty. But what about engagement?

Again, because self-styled reformers at the state and federal levels have been so busy building remote-control accountability systems, we know little about what school systems built on the principle of engagement might look like. There is, however, one exception. One unlikely state, smack in the middle of the country, has developed a school improvement system—in this state, no one talks of reform; people prefer to think of all schools as engaged in school improvement—that turns traditional conceptions of accountability inside out. In doing so, it helps us to evaluate this engagement idea, to examine what it does and what it renders.

In 1998, Nebraska became the forty-eighth state in the nation to adopt state standards in core content areas. Two years later, it became the forty-ninth state to adopt a state assessment and accountability system. By this time, Nebraska had witnessed the pitfalls of systems based on state tests. It also wished to honor the state's long tradition of local control and signal its faith in its educators. And so it chose to give districts discretion about how they met state standards, including the assessments they would use to measure student learning. It designed a *statewide system of local assessments*—the School-based, Teacher-led Assessment and Reporting System (STARS). Although this system includes some checks—a standardized writing assessment and occasional reporting on national standardized tests—districts for the most part use locally designed assessments to measure and report student performance. They are also responsible for documenting the quality of those assessments. The state evaluates district portfolios based on reviews of both student performance *and* the technical quality of the district's assessment process.

I describe both the story and the components of STARS in detail in Chapter 3; here it is enough to suggest that Nebraska's approach differs from what we find in other states in several important ways:

◆ It is a system of local assessments, not a state test.

◆ It requires multiple measures of student performance.

◆ It requires documentation of assessment quality.

◆ It uses classroom-based assessments for state reporting.

◆ It includes no high-stakes tests.

Nebraska's education commissioner, Douglas Christensen (2001a), has described STARS as "bottom up"; that is, the locus of the system is the classroom, where the most important decisions about teaching and learning take place. The principle here is that assessment must be meaningful and useful in the first instance to teachers and students. So another way to think about STARS is as an inside-out system: teachers weave assessment into teaching and learning in the classroom first and *then* share the information obtained from those activities with others.

The Nebraska Story features teachers and administrators redefining what it means to be a professional educator, schools remaking themselves into professional learning communities, and a state developing new lenses for and conversations about the work of schools. To be sure, the plot is a complicated one: The road to school improvement and improved student learning in Nebraska has not been (nor is it now, five years into the process) smooth or painless. And it's fair to say that the still-young STARS needs time to mature. But at the end of the day, the most important plot element of the Nebraska Story is foreshadowing: put simply, STARS gives us a glimpse into the next generation of standards, assessment, and "accountability"—the first twenty-first-century approach to school improvement.

Design of the Book

Most good stories, engaging stories, are character driven. The protagonist of the Nebraska Story is *teachers*. Or better: teacher-leaders. I will judge this book to be successful if it helps teachers take a more active leadership role in their schools' efforts to support student learning. If it helps teachers lead the way toward twenty-first-century school "reform," all the better. But in the meantime, the Nebraska experience provides a range of more humble, but undoubtedly significant, lessons for teachers anywhere.

Chapter 2 describes the accountability agenda, counts its considerable costs, and begins to outline an alternative approach to school improvement: engagement.

Chapter 3 shares big-picture research on Nebraska's School-based, Teacher-led Assessment and Reporting System (STARS). It provides an overview of statewide results but also some of the key cultural changes in Nebraska schools since the advent of STARS. In so doing, this chapter shows not only *that* a system based on the notion of engagement is possible, but also what it does and what it renders.

Chapters 4–6 are organized around how Nebraska educators build rich, engaged relationships with various educational partners. Each of these chapters includes both an overview of trends in Nebraska schools and at least one portrait of practice in which Nebraska educators highlight a key practice from their classroom or school. Chapter 4 demonstrates how Nebraska teachers are making assessment meaningful in their classrooms both by sharing assessment information with students and by *involving* them in assessment. Chapter 5 demonstrates how Nebraska teachers are developing new models of professional development that bring them out of what they call "private practice" in order to work together across content areas and grade levels. Chapter 6 demonstrates how Nebraska teachers are building school-community relationships that support and sustain school improvement. Taken together, these chapters provide a kind of primer on the arts of teacher leadership. My brief conclusion offers a final call for teacher-leaders to set a new agenda for twenty-first-century public education.

Notes

1. I am grateful to Peter H. Johnston (1992) for this formulation.

2. See *Quality Counts* reports at www.edweek.org/re/articles/2004/10/15/qc-archives.html.

3. This phrase was a mainstay of then-Governor Bush's 2000 election bid. See, for instance, the transcript of his first debate with Al Gore, available at the Commission on Presidential Debates website: www.debates.org/pages/trans2000a.html.

4. My thinking here is informed by the philosophical tradition of pragmatism. According to Louis Menand (2001) in his wonderful book *The Metaphysical Club*, pragmatists understand ideas to be "provisional responses to particular and unreproducible circumstances." Therefore, "their survival depends not on their immutability but on their adaptability" (xii).

Accountability and After

The ride from Lincoln to the reservation becomes increasingly treacherous. By the time I cross the bridge onto the reservation itself, the swirling wind is pelting snow against my windshield and nudging my small car first left, then right. I pass several pickup trucks and silently applaud their owners' choice of vehicle. When I left Lincoln two hours ago, it was a beautiful, sun-shiny, late-winter day. Here, the weather is punishing and the land seems to show it. Leafless trees have assumed a permanently crouched position, tall grasses lie flat beneath sheaths of ice, and even the hills seem somehow beaten down, rounded by the fierce wind.

And yet, there's a kind of beauty to the place: a starkness, a spareness, an openness. Over the rolling hills, I can see to the horizon in all directions.

Finally, I pull into the small town at the center of the reservation. It is not difficult to find the public school; it is by far the most modern building. Not that there are many buildings to begin with: I see a gas station, a church, a small grocery store, another shop whose business is unclear to me, and a handful of small houses. I see no people.

As I turn off the car engine, I think about what Mr. Sands,[1] the high school principal, has told me about the place:

Unemployment: 75%

Number of students, K–12: approximately 400 (usually)

Students transferring in or out of school each year (mobility): 50%

Percentage of students receiving free or reduced lunch: 99%

Families receiving daily newspaper: less than 5%

Families with telephone service: less than 50%

Homes with more than a handful of books: a few, maybe

Number of days the school sends out a van to check on kids whom the staff have no way of contacting: every day

I wonder how long I should wait. It is 9:40; I am twenty minutes early. After a moment's thought, I head in: it's too cold to sit out here.

A new wing is being added to this K–12 building; it will house the high school. Mr. Sands is excited, not only because it will afford the high school more room but also because it will house new amenities such as a culture center, a computer lab, and a large open space for circle time. Mr. Sands, drawing on a tribal tradition, imagines convening the high schoolers in the open area each morning for sharing and reflection.

Despite the plastic tarps hanging from the ceiling and the ladders, buckets, and tools leaning neatly against the wall, the building is bright and colorful, decorated with kids' artwork and posters displaying "Native Pride." A huge glass case greets visitors; it is filled with trophies, ribbons, and photographs of athletic teams and academic achievers. As usual, I learn a great deal about what is important to this school within thirty seconds of my arrival. Scanning the foyer and hallway leading to the main office, I learn two things about this school: (1) it puts kids first, and (2) it honors the kids' culture.

A friendly office staff member advises me that Mr. Sands is on his way. I may wait for him in the library, where I will find coffee.

The library is well appointed: it has several walls and stacks of books, a few computers, and a couple of copy machines. I take a seat at one of the wooden tables and sip my coffee. As I fish around in my book bag for the tape recorder and tapes I will need for my interviews, several students come in and speak with the librarian in familiar, comfortable tones. Once they leave, the librarian, a middle-aged white woman, tells me a perversely funny story about mice getting stuck in one of the copy machines.

Although I have never met him, I have no trouble recognizing Mr. Sands when he enters the library. Unlike the kids, almost 100 percent of whom are Native American, much of the teaching staff is white. Even so, this big white man with a booming voice (and, it turns out, a killer handshake) stands out. He has the kind of physical presence that fills a room, and the fact that he oozes self-confidence, always looking his interlocutor in the eye, doesn't diminish the effect any.

Mr. Sands escorts me to his office, where we conduct the interview. Like the foyer and hallways, his office is heavily decorated—almost overdecorated, so dizzying is the effect—with students' work. Several dream catchers are strung from the ceiling; Mr. Sands' closely cropped hair just clears them.

I am mid–first question when the telephone rings the first time. Holding up an index finger, Mr. Sands answers it, barks several one-word answers into the phone, and ends the conversation with a brisk but not unfriendly "Do it!"

I begin to ask the question again and he moves to his computer. "Gotta do this," he explains, composing an email. I give him a no-big-deal shoulder shrug. By the time the interview ends an hour and a half later, I will be an expert in this gesture: Mr. Sands multitasks through the entire interview, taking more phone calls, answering his door several times to handle office problems, and sending emails. At one point, a school board member stops by to say hello. Then it's a parent. Finally, a former student. And yet, through all this, Mr. Sands is somehow attentive to my questions and offers thoughtful, articulate answers.

Mr. Sands told me over the phone that all students in his school develop portfolios of their work. Students design the portfolios themselves, choosing what to include (within guidelines) and reflecting on their learning in the different subject areas. Teachers' assessments of students' portfolios are used for state reporting, but that is not—Mr. Sands is adamant on this point— their primary purpose.

Why portfolios, then? Mr. Sands: "To me, it's a mark of the people who live here. Tests aren't the important thing. [They want to know,] What can you really do? Well, we've said [to the students,] 'Here, show us what you can do.' [And] portfolios mean something to our students. When they open it up, there's a meaning to that. When you fill in bubbles on a sheet or look at simply numbers on a page, sometimes that doesn't have the meaning because it's like, 'I'm not sure that's really mine.' You know, there's a craftsmanship in this culture and…*[he motions around his office]* look at my artwork. This is craftsmanship…A bubble on a sheet isn't craftsmanship. [But a portfolio is] a measure our kids buy in to because that's craftsmanship, just like making blankets and moccasins and arrowheads."

I ask Mr. Sands how the portfolios are evaluated. He explains that the school follows the model of an "architectural review." That is, the students present their portfolios to teachers and to a group of invited guests— "significant people from the community," including parents, elders, and school board members—and then the guests ask questions and provide comments on the quality of the presentation. He explains that this process is much more meaningful to the community and the kids than a test score ever could be.

The teachers I talk to throughout the day agree. Each talks about connecting academic work to the kids' culture. The literacy teacher, for example, talks about how exciting it is for the kids to be learning the tribe's native language. Their cultural pride, she tells me, carries over into all of their work. Though they did have trouble with the statewide assessment last year, she confides. The prompt asked students to write about the wisdom of after-school jobs for high schoolers. To these kids, after-school jobs are a foreign concept; there are no jobs for them on the reservation. Still, she believes in the importance of writing arguments—of helping kids gain a voice in their communities—and so she wrote a persuasive essay arguing that basketball should be banned from school: the lights are expensive, the kids should be doing homework, and so on. Then she challenged the students to write their own essays taking the opposite position, which they readily did, because they are "fanatical" about basketball. The result? After several drafts, they produced strong arguments that looked nothing like the writing they produced for the state assessment. The key, their teacher emphasizes, is simple: connect writing with "what kids care about."

Later in the day, Mr. Sands brings me to a small room at the back of the building where the portfolios of students who have graduated or otherwise left are stored. Before we get there, Mr. Sands introduces me to a student and asks him to explain to me how he is putting together his graduation portfolio. Clearly shy, the boy demurs. But Mr. Sands is persistent. Through gentle but direct questioning, he helps the boy through his explanation. Slightly embarrassed, I thank the student. Mr. Sands asks him to return to class and the boy heads off, visibly relieved but with what I think is the trace of a smile.

The room that houses the portfolios is cramped and windowless; it's little more than a storage closet. Portfolios are stacked everywhere. Some are plain: binders filled with math problems, essays, science lab notes, and so on. Others are beautifully designed. One has pencil sketches on the cover. Another sports a feather beneath the plastic sheath. A third is decorated with what appears to be artful graffiti.

I ask Mr. Sands how long the school will keep these portfolios. I am not sure at first that he hears my question.

Finally, quietly: "These don't belong to me or the school; they belong to the kids. In a way, they *are* the kids." He waits a moment, apparently allowing the weight of the comment to settle. Then: "Do you throw kids out? No, you do not."

———————•◆•———————

Mr. Sands' school is one of my favorite places to visit. It is full of warm, smart people who genuinely like kids. It is not nearly as well equipped as many schools I have visited, but it is nonetheless a cheerful, welcoming place always buzzing with activity. Each time I visit the school, I walk away energized and inspired. In the face of dire challenges, this school is thriving.

And yet, at the time of the visit I just recounted, the school was, according to federal accountability measures, failing—or, to use their unfortunate term, "in need of improvement" (what school is not in need of improvement?). I suspect this won't come as a surprise to teachers. They won't be shocked to learn that between 65 percent and 75 percent of students at this school score below the U.S. average on annual reading and math tests. They won't be taken aback when I suggest that this school has a very difficult time reaching minimum assessment participation requirements. They won't blink an eye at the low graduate rates compared with the rest of this largely white state. How could any of this be otherwise, considering the social and economic struggles the reservation faces as a result of a long legacy of systemic, racist exploitation and neglect?

In truth, I think most teachers would be floored by the amazing achievements of this school. The kids are in school. They are learning. Their achievement *is* improving—significantly, in some areas. Attendance and graduation rates are increasing. The kids are reconnecting with their native culture, including their tribal language, which few of them speak. They care about their schoolwork, including their portfolios. And so do their teachers, their families, and the tribal elders, many of whom pass daily through the open doors of the school. A status check will do little more than confirm the school's challenges; on any measure that matters, however, the school is indeed improving.

The problem with what traditional accountability measures tell us about this school is not just that they don't account for the ways in which the school *is* accountable despite its less than stellar bottom-line numbers—though that's true. Rather, it's that the whole idea of test-based accountability is at best beside the point and at worst a threat to the good things happening in this school. Imagine, for instance, if Mr. Sands and his colleagues decided to expend the bulk of their energies trying to raise students' scores on standardized tests. I suspect, given their enormous energy, commitment, and talent, that they could do it. But at what price? What would happen, for instance, to the culturally rich curriculum that could never be reflected in such a test? What would happen to the student portfolios? To circle time and the study of the native language? To staff and student morale? Would Mr. Sands stop students in the hall and ask them to explain their test scores to visitors? Would parents, community members, and school board members continue to drop by to say hello? And what would this say to the community, which, after all, values craftsmanship, not test scores?

In other words, the problem here is not that accountability asks too much of this school; it's that it asks too little. The relationship between this school and this community is not defined by a trade of tax dollars for test scores. It is defined by reciprocity and a mutually responsible partnership. Educators and community members alike demand more than a number on a spreadsheet; instead, they ask the students, "What can you really do?" And they show up to hear, deliberate on, and evaluate the answer.

The rich forms of engagement we see in Mr. Sands' school are all too rare. The accountability agenda, sadly, is making them rarer still. By focusing the attention of educators and communities on bottom-line numbers rather than human relationships, accountability reduces schooling to a spectator sport. It leaves noneducators unsure about how to participate in the schools in their communities and it leaves schools unsure about how to invite that participation. Indeed, its cold metrics often promote mutual distrust, driving a wedge between schools and their communities.

My purpose in this chapter is to count the cost of accountability and to propose another approach to school improvement, one that would seek to protect and enhance the dialogue-rich relationships we see both inside Mr. Sands' school and between the school and the community. I do not propose to provide a thorough explication or critique of the federal No Child Left Behind Act; others have capably dissected what Gerald Bracey (2003) terms this "weapon of mass destruction" (see Marshak 2003; Neill 2003; Neill et al. 2004; Noguera 2004; Sadker and Zittleman 2004; and Kohn 2004b). Instead, I intend to show how NCLB exemplifies and consolidates what I call the accountability agenda. It's important to think about accountability as an agenda because although its proponents present it as mere common sense, it is neither natural nor inevitable. In fact, it is the byword of a coordinated, pernicious campaign that serves corporate interests at the expense of teachers, students, and communities.

A Short History of a Bad Idea

Although NCLB is surely the most ambitious and intrusive federal accountability legislation in U.S. history, the accountability agenda long predates the signing of the law in 2002 by President George W. Bush. The idea of accountability rose to prominence among reformers during the educational and literacy "crises" of the 1970s. As that decade began, education writer John Morris predicted "the dawning of the age of accountability" (Hunt 2005, 86). Back-to-basics educational tracts like Leon Lessinger's *Every Kid a Winner* (1970) and Paul Copperman's *Literacy Hoax* (1978) bore out Morris' notion. So did a series of alarmist pieces in the mid-1970s in the popular press. In 1975, for instance, *Newsweek* ran a cover story titled "Why Johnny Can't Read."

That same year, the U.S. Office of Education sponsored and issued the Adult Performance Study, which found that more than 20 percent of U.S. adults were functionally illiterate. In 1977, an advisory panel headed by former secretary of labor William Wirtz issued a report on the decline of SAT scores (cited in Flesch 1981). All these cries of crisis encouraged self-styled reformers to call for greater accountability from public schools. This era saw a variety of technocratic management techniques imported from business into schools, including performance contracts (often with private firms), management by objectives, and zero-based budgeting (Tyack 1974). It also saw a dramatic increase in the use of standardized tests to measure student and school performance.[2]

The 1980s were ushered in by more of the same. In 1981, Rudolf Flesch, who had authored the 1955 tract *Why Johnny Can't Read*, announced that Johnny *still* couldn't read. And then, in 1983, President Reagan's Commission on Excellence in Education issued *A Nation at Risk*. If the rhetoric of crisis of the 1970s seemed extreme, it paled in comparison to this report, which opened this way:

> Our Nation is at risk. Our once unchalleng[ed] preeminence in commerce, industry, science, and technological innovation is being overtaken by competitors throughout the world. . . . If an unfriendly foreign power had attempted to impose on America the mediocre educational performance that exists today, we might well have viewed it as an act of war. As it stands, we have allowed this to happen to ourselves. We have even squandered the gains in student achievement made in the wake of the Sputnik challenge. . . . We have, in effect, been committing an act of unthinking, unilateral educational disarmament.

The Commission—whose membership included corporate CEOs, higher education representatives, state and local education officials, and exactly one teacher—sent a clear message: Educational standards are too low and rigor must be reestablished in order to compete in the global marketplace. Among the recommendations of the committee, not surprisingly, was a call for standardized achievement tests at key educational moments, especially at the conclusion of high school.

A Nation at Risk has cast a long shadow over educational reform during the past two decades. Its key precepts were certainly in evidence during the education summit of the nation's governors convened by President George H. W. Bush and led by then-governor of Arkansas Bill Clinton in 1989. And so were the principles of the Business Roundtable (BRT), an immensely powerful—indeed, seemingly ubiquitous—lobbying group whose distinctive mark can be found on almost every popular reform idea these days, including many of those enshrined in NCLB. Most notably, the BRT—which boasts among its two hundred members the heads of forty-two of the top fifty largest Fortune 500 firms, as well as most of the important leaders in commercial banking, insurance, retail chains, transportation companies, and utilities companies—advocates state standards and standardized state tests, rewards and sanctions based on test scores, and intensive, teacher-directed phonics instruction in the early grades. The BRT has the ear of policy makers and media alike, and it does not shy away from trumpeting its agenda (Emery and Ohanian 2004, 114).

Influenced by *A Nation at Risk* and by the BRT, the 1989 summit generated a set of national education goals, including incentives and disincentives for school "performance" as measured on standardized tests. These accountability provisions were enshrined in Bush's America 2000 policy, which included, among other things, a call for a "voluntary" national test. Congress rejected the latter proposal, but Bill Clinton resurrected the idea in his 1997 State of the Union speech, in which he outlined a "crusade" for educational standards. Clinton's testing proposal, too, died in Congress, but his Goals 2000 package and the 1994 Educate America Act placed accountability at the center of the school reform agenda by tying school performance to federal aid.

President George W. Bush's education agenda stands on the shoulders of this bipartisan effort, which was heavily influenced by the nation's business community and its commitment to improving America's competitiveness in the global marketplace (Sacks 1999, 80–81). But the president's agenda is also a revamped version of the Texas accountability model developed (but not initiated) under Bush's governorship. Many NCLB requirements are very similar to those in the Texas system, including greater parental "choice," increased emphasis on reading (especially for young children), and a slew of accountability requirements, including state standards, annual student testing, and consequences for districts and schools that fail to reach annual progress objectives.

One of the most striking features of the Texas accountability model in the 1980s and 1990s was the heavy hand of business. For instance, billionaire H. Ross Perot—with a headline-grabbing announcement that the only way to change Texas schools was to "nuke them"—set about reforming the schools through business management techniques (McNeil 2000, 153, 179). He was aided by the Texas Business and Education Coalition as well as Texans for Education, both organizations established to help business leaders influence state education policy. Together, these reformers pushed an agenda that included state standards, curriculum alignment to standards, site-based management of schools, annual testing in grades 1–11, punishments for schools and districts that were not "performing," and contracts with school management organizations to run "failing" schools. They also succeeded in increasing the influence of business interests in local school board membership and educational policy, including in future U.S. commissioner of education Rod Paige's Houston, where curriculum was taken out of the hands of teachers and prepackaged into narrowly conceived "proficiencies," which were to be taught in lockstep fashion. A management consultant even designed a set of "observable, measurable" behaviors for Houston teachers, including having a catchy opener, making eye contact with students, writing the objectives of the lesson on the board, having closure at the end of the lesson, and so on (McNeil 2000, 221).

The spirit of the accountability agenda in Texas is perhaps best captured by an adviser to Governor Bush, who told a group of community members that while he wasn't "against democracy *per se*," it would not work in education because "[w]hat you need in education is a power board—of business executives—the right people in the community—then your board brings in a few experts and the experts will advise them on a plan" (McNeil 2000, 268). This expert-reliant mentality has now taken the national stage, creating a platform for corporate CEOs such as Perot, Bill Gates, and Louis Gerstner to use their celebrity—and, often, their indignation at "the education establishment"—to shape the education reform conversation around their worldviews. For instance, Gerstner, former CEO of IBM, writes in his coauthored book *Reinventing Education* that "ultimate accountability for schools" is possible only "by meeting a market test: satisfying customers" (Gerstner et al. 1994, 46). Like other business-minded reformers, Gerstner insists that public schooling is best treated as an individualized commodity: a product proffered on an open market for individual customers (students, parents, employers, taxpayers), rather than a public trust.

Indeed, today's reformers often bypass the analogy—schools are *like* businesses—and pursue outright privatization of public schooling. Some observers have argued (convincingly, in my view) that NCLB is a thinly veiled push for privatization.[3] In any event, the increasing influence of privatizers on public education is not difficult to detect. Entire urban districts (Philadelphia's, for instance) are contracted out to for-profit management companies such as Edison

Schools Incorporated. Private educational management organizations are a boom industry. Schools and programs are sponsored by corporations. Children are barraged by commercial advertisements as they walk the school hallways or sit in the stands at their schools' athletic fields—or even as they sit in their classrooms (thanks to Channel One, the program that provides technology to schools in return for the airing of commercials). Kindergartners take standardized tests produced by private companies operating at a considerable profit. Educational policy is increasingly influenced by think tanks such as the American Enterprise Institute, The Heritage Foundation, and Chester Finn's Fordham Foundation, by organizations such as Phyllis Schlafly's Eagle Forum and the Business Roundtable, and by initiatives such as William Bennett's Campaign for America's Children.[4] What all these conservative groups and initiatives have in common is a pro-voucher, proprivatization, probusiness approach to school reform through accountability.

Counting the Costs of Accountability

The accountability agenda, then, is a *coordinated campaign* by a small but powerful set of interest groups.[5] And yet, this agenda is promoted under the guise of common sense and wrapped in warm platitudes that sound all-American and even democratic: all kids can learn; we must level the playing field; we must have high expectations for all American children; we must not leave children behind. But despite its seemingly high-minded invocations of democracy, the discourse of account-ability reduces that concept to a narrowly economic concern with getting one's money's worth in a competitive "free market" of goods and services (Apple 1993, 2001).

There's a perverse irony in the accountability agenda. While it extols the virtues of economy and efficiency and posits all alternatives as pie-in-the-sky dreaming, it is itself unreasonable, enormously costly, and incredibly wasteful. Let me take a page from the accountability book and count the ways.

Educational Costs

The most obvious educational cost of test-based accountability is the school time given over to testing rather than teaching. Each year around the country, teachers and students interrupt teaching and learning to devote hours and hours to testing and test preparation. While this development is surely a boon for the standardized testing and test-prep industries, which together take in billions of dollars annually,[6] it robs teachers and students of valuable classroom experiences.

And this serious problem is only the tip of a rather imposing iceberg. Linda McNeil's (2000) research on "legislated learning" in Texas offers a vivid portrait of more systemic educational costs. McNeil found that as Perot's standardized, management-oriented methods were employed in formerly autonomous schools, the quality of teaching declined dramatically. Richly conceived lessons and projects were shelved in favor of the regimented, fragmented curriculum handed to teachers by the districts. As educators around the country have learned, standardized curricula and standardized tests lead to a narrowing of curriculum and a focus on lower-order, easily tested skills (Darling-Hammond 1997; Henning-Stout 1994; Neill et al. 2004; Kohn 1999, 2000; Posner 2004).

Of course, teachers don't enter the profession in order to prep kids for tests. When they are de-skilled in this way, we see yet another educational cost. They engage in what McNeil calls "defensive teaching," which means that they strike a deal with students: I won't ask much of you, and you won't give me any grief. Teachers and students alike drift into compliance mode, which allows them to peacefully coexist but meanwhile steadily erodes the quality of their relationship. Many studies suggest that teachers' sense of their own professionalism suffers in tightly controlled environments and that this has a negative effect on students' learning environment.[7] Meanwhile, the high stakes attached to tests create immense anxieties for teachers and students. In response, many teachers resort to cheating (coaching kids or changing their answers)—or leave the profession. For their part, students—predictably—handle their anxieties in a variety of ways . . . including becoming physically ill while taking tests.[8]

The accountability agenda entails other educational costs as well. For instance, assessments that actually help students and teachers make good decisions in classrooms are sacrificed in favor of tests designed solely for accountability purposes, even though the latter are often of questionable quality, are (not coincidentally) designed by for-profit corporations rather than by educators, and are consistently misinterpreted and misused (Beadie 2004; Haney, Madaus, and Lyons 1993; Linn 2000; Meier 2002; Kohn 1999, 2000; Sacks 1999). This is particularly disheartening when we consider the wealth of evidence that effective formative, classroom-based assessments improve learning (Black et al. 2004; Black and Wiliam 1998; Guskey 2003; Stiggins 2004a). And on top of this, recent comparisons of states with and without high-stakes testing indicate these testing regimes don't even do what they are intended to do: raise achievement levels (Reeves 2002; Amrein and Berliner 2003).

Most disturbing of all, test-based accountability costs us the opportunity to improve the learning of our most vulnerable kids. In fact, education for poor and minority children is actually getting much worse in standardized, test-focused schools. Kids who have traditionally done least well on standardized tests are given the most intense test preparation by the least qualified teachers. As a result, those children who are most in need of rich, engaged teaching are least likely to receive it (Darling-Hammond 1997; Kohn 1999; Kozol 2005; Reeves 2002; Wood 2004). Instead, their schools are turned into test-prep centers. Linda McNeil, quite properly, calls this kind of educational malpractice a "new form of discrimination" (2000, xxi).

What most ails schools is not what President Bush calls "the soft bigotry of low expectations"; it's the hard bigotry of systemic inequality. Demanding that all kids be pronounced proficient on an arbitrary timetable, giving all kids the same test, punishing schools that do not make "adequate yearly progress" (AYP)—these accountability measures suggest that we can simply *will* (or be forced into) a miracle.[9] But they do nothing to improve education for these young people. Worse yet, they draw attention away from policies and programs that might have a chance to do so by redistributing talented teachers, fixing broken school aid formulas, stanching the resegregation of the schools, building sustainable partnerships with communities, and so on.

Social Costs

We *could* address the social challenges to public education. But that would mean taking a hard look at poverty and racism in this country and coming up with real solutions like universal preschool, needs-based school funding formulas, new school buildings in poor communities staffed by the best teachers we can recruit, reintegration of resegregated urban schools, and so on. Instead, we rely on accountability measures that have no record of success in turning schools around and in fact have an ever growing record of failure.[10] Among those failures is a raft of socially deleterious trends: increasing (but underreported) dropout rates; decreasing (but overreported) graduation rates; growing student attrition or retention in grades preceding high-stakes testing grades; and widespread educator cheating scandals (Benton and Hacker 2004; Lyn 2005; "Houston Schools" 2005;

Dobbs 2003; Goldberg 2005; Myatt and Kemp 2004; Ohanian 2003; Goldhaber and Hannaway 2004; Linn 2000; Wheelock 2003).

Subtler, perhaps, but equally important is this social cost: the sacrifice of a rich public discussion about the purposes and functions of public schools. Accountability hawks purposely silence teachers and students with their relentless assault on "the education establishment."[11] As journalist Peter Sacks suggests, the American public is continually pounded with the message that teachers can't be trusted and that the answer is "[m]ore standards, more reform, more accountability...[and a]bove all, more standardized testing" (1999, 69). And despite ample evidence that educational achievement in American schools has *not*, in fact, declined even as the schools have served an increasingly diverse population (Berliner and Biddle 1995; Bracey 2002; Kohn 2000), this campaign is working. In an annual Phi Delta Kappa/Gallup poll, for instance, respondents consistently give "the nation's schools" much lower marks than the schools in their own communities and especially the schools their own children attend.[12]

A key precept of this campaign to sow seeds of distrust in public school teachers is that teachers' low expectations are to blame for the failings of the schools. Former U.S. assistant secretary of education Chester Finn, for instance, offers the following diagnosis:

> The public schools system as we know it has proved that it cannot reform itself. It is an ossified government monopoly that functions largely for the benefit of its employees and interest groups rather than that of children and taxpayers. American education needs a radical overhaul. For starters, control over education must be shifted into the hands of parents and true reformers—people who will insist on something altogether different than murmuring excuses for the catastrophe that surrounds us (Bracey 2002, ix).

Similarly, S. Paul Reville, a businessman and active player in Massachusetts school reforms, explains that the controversial, high-stakes Massachusetts Comprehensive Assessment System was put into place "to dislodge the low expectations that characterize the status quo and result in the widely disparate impact of our current ineffective and unequal system of public schooling" (2004, 594). Like Finn, Reville identifies educators as the problem; it is their low expectations that create inequity. So reform can come only from the outside, in this case (surprise!) from corporate interests.

Of course, there is rhetorical power in positioning oneself as coura-geously opposing a mighty but wrongheaded establishment. Whether they are calling teachers and their organizations obstructionists, pro-gressives,[13] or even terrorists—as former U.S. commissioner of educa-tion Rod Paige called the National Education Association—these reformers send a clear message: *Teachers are powerful; they are hiding something; do not trust them.* They position themselves and their audi-ences as victims of powerful vested interests, playing a disingenuous game of insider/outsider: *We* want what's best for kids; *they* want to feather their nests, to protect their perks. This rhetorical move is itself a power grab—an attempt, namely, to silence teachers' voices.

Moreover, although I don't have space to elaborate in detail here, this rhetorical move must be understood within the larger context of the derogation of women's voices and women's work. Various writers have established the connection between the gendered hierarchy of school and cultural assumptions about women as pliable, obedient, and imbued with an ethic of care (Tyack 1974; Darling-Hammond 1997; Marshall 2004). That is, women have been recruited to teach precisely because they are viewed as compliant and naturally nurtur-ing. This has allowed mostly male "experts"—administrators, policy-makers, politicians—to run the educational show from a distance. In public education, planning (the province of men) is routinely sev-ered from execution (the province of women). In any event, teachers rarely have a voice in the design or function of the educational insti-tutions in which they make their living. The accountability agenda chokes off dialogue and degrades those who spend their days with children. We all lose when "common sense" stands in for reasoned public deliberation and the airing of diverse viewpoints.

Human Costs

This third category, human costs, is in a sense redundant. Because edu-cation is a human endeavor, I've been talking all along about human costs. But I want to underscore that we are not talking about dry-as-dust policies and discourses; we are talking about deeply personal values and experiences. When the accountability agenda removes control of education from the hands of those closest to that human interaction—teachers and students—and when it further denies them a voice in the conversation and decision-making around that endeavor, it robs them of precious human freedoms: to exercise one's intellect, to inquire, to imagine, to wonder, to develop the capacities of discernment and judg-ment, to make decisions about one's own learning, to speak. Perhaps tightly controlled, top-down businesses don't need, or even want, people who do these things; a few experts can carry this load. But democracy does need people who do these things.

And schools need people who do these things. They need expert teachers, not expert technocrats who tell teachers what to do. They need teachers who know their subject and also know how to teach, not "emergency certified" people who have not been trained in colleges of education.[14] By granting remote "experts" control over education while denying professional status to teachers, we deprive teachers of their human vocation. In turn, we deprive students, their families, and their communities the considerable expertise of this group of people who have dedicated their lives to helping others learn. The human cost, then, could not be higher. We are sacrificing the heart and soul of education: *engagement*. Built on distrust and a stern-father morality, the accountability agenda in fact fosters precisely the opposite: disengagement—between teachers and students, between schools and teachers, between schools and students, and between schools and communities.

Teachers, students, and communities deserve better than the top-down, carrot-and-stick approach of the accountability agenda. They deserve schools that are places where people want to be, where human freedoms are protected and nourished, where what we say and think and feel matters to other people who in turn matter to us, where we learn to work on and work out the most important questions and challenges we face.

After Accountability: What's Next?

Accountability can never help schools become those kinds of places— even if this were its goal, which it is not—because it is premised on the severely constricted model of the commercial transaction: getting what you pay for and paying for what you get. For all the boisterous bluster surrounding it—*all kids proficient by 2014 or else*—the accountability agenda is a flimsy house of cards poised to tumble. In schools and homes and town halls and state legislatures and universities across the country, the high costs and scarce rewards of the accountability agenda are causing considerable unrest. People are seeing what it does and what it renders, and they are hungry for a new idea, a new approach, a new way of thinking about schools and schooling.

Fortunately, this new idea is taking shape. It lurks in the pages of school reform literature. It haunts staff rooms and classrooms. It emboldens the resistance to high-stakes testing we see around the country. It is even, as I will show in the next chapter, being tested in one state's assessment system.

The principles of this new idea are far from startling (especially to teachers), but they take us about as far from the accountability agenda as we could get. The thinking goes like this: Meaningful, sustainable school improvement requires strong *relationships*. These relationships are forged through conversation. They are nurtured within a community of learning marked by shared commitment among educational partners. They foster teacher leadership because teachers are leaders of learning. They are reciprocal because real teaching and learning require mutual responsibility. They are premised, in a word, on *engagement* (see Figure 2–1).

I have described some features of engagement already; others I will take up in later chapters. Here, note that this alternative model challenges the most basic premise of accountability: that public schools are failing and must be reformed from the outside through the implementation of business protocols and marketization. Instead, it posits that *all* schools can improve by building their internal capacity through committed, mutually responsible partnerships.

Two Ideas of School Reform	
Accountability	**Engagement**
Business model	Democratic model
School reform	School improvement
Teachers as impediments to reform	Teachers as leaders of school improvement
One-way relationships	Mutual relationships
Student achievement	Student learning
Test based	Assessment informed
Standardization	Standards
Stern-father morality	Shared-responsibility ethic
Transaction	Interaction
Top-down	Bottom-up (or inside out)
Exerts control	Builds capacity
High stakes	High impact
Unearned distrust	Earned trust
Competition	Collaboration
Compliance	Commitment
Assessment *of* learning (only)	Assessment *for* learning (also)
Demands simplicity	Embraces complexity

Figure 2–1 Two Ideas of School Reform

The verb *engage* has three relevant meanings: (1) to attract, (2) to involve, and (3) to take on or confront. Engaging schools *attract* the interest of students, teachers, and other educational partners; they are places where we want to spend time. They also *involve* deliberation by citizens on matters of public importance. And they help us *confront* the complexities of democratic living; they are places where we work on and work out the most challenging questions and problems that we face as democratic citizens. To be engaged is to be richly involved in an activity, to have taken it on. It is not doing the minimum required of you by a *trans*action; it is doing what you ought to do by virtue of your understanding of an *inter*action. This is the spirit, the disposition, the commitment that must drive schooling.

Of course, engagement alone will not solve all of our problems in schools, just as schools alone cannot solve all of our social problems. But the hope of democracy is that public deliberation and shared decision making are the best approach to persistent social problems. In the engagement model, schools are incubators of democratic dialogue. As Deborah Meier suggests, "[k]ids learn the art of democratic conversation—and the art of passing judgment—by watching and talking to teachers whom the larger community shows respect for and who in turn show respect for their communities" (2002, 4). Mr. Sands would agree. Democratic conversation is the hallmark of his school. It is a place where students, teachers, and community members feel that what they have to say matters. A place they want to be. A place of belonging—but also a frequently uncomfortable place: a place where tough challenges are confronted and where hard decisions are made. An engaging place.

Notes

1. I use a pseudonym to protect this interviewee's confidentiality.

2. Of course, the 1970s were not the first time business models, practices, and criteria were applied to schools. As historians such as Callahan (1962), Cremin (1961), Spring (1990), Tyack (1974), and Tyack and Cuban (1995) have demonstrated, many of the most enduring features of the modern school—including standardized curriculum, assessment, and instruction, strictly regimented time (punctuated by bells, no less), mobile students but stationary teachers, school boards modeled on corporate structures—were borrowed from factories and businesses in the late nineteenth and early twentieth centuries. Callahan asserts that the business model was standardized in American education by 1925 (1962, 6).

3. Under NCLB guidelines, consequences for schools labeled "in need of improvement" include allowing parents to use their share of federal dollars to purchase open-market supplemental services, contracting schools out to private management companies, and appointing outside "experts" to advise schools. President Bush is on record as supporting vouchers for parents of public school children who wish to move their kids to private schools. Charter schools, meanwhile, are increasingly managed by for-profit "educational management organizations." On NCLB and privatization, see Bracey (2004) and Kohn (2004a, 2004b).

4. On the influence of conservative thought on current educational policy and practice, see Apple (1993, 2001), Bracey (2002), Emery and Ohanian (2004), and Shor (1986).

5. Although these interest groups have allied, they have somewhat varying agendas. Some are corporate-minded true believers in open markets in all spheres of public life, some are part of a new class of technocrats with no particular interest in public education per se, and still others are evangelicals dedicated to "returning" God to the schools. See Apple (2001).

6. It is difficult to obtain reliable figures on the profits of these industries; testing and test-preparation companies are notoriously secretive on this matter. Peter Sacks (1999) reports that Americans take between 200 million and 600 million tests per year. He claims that by 1997, standardized achievement test sales for K–12 alone were almost $200 million. Of course, these tests are only a slice of a much larger pie. Surely that number is much higher today, especially with the recent acceleration of computer-based testing. And that number doesn't include test preparation, which Crystal England (2003) estimates to have taken in $2.5 billion in recent years. See also Haney, Madaus, and Lyons (1993); Kohn (2000); and Pyle (2005).

7. Hargreaves et al. cite multiple studies conducted in England and Wales that reveal that prescriptive environments led teachers to feel less confident, "cynically compliant," and depressed (2001, 6). Similarly, Patricia Wasley found that teachers in controlled environments in turn became controlling themselves—as well as isolated from and distrustful of their colleagues (1991, 92–99).

8. Researchers Audrey Amrein and David Berliner found that high-stakes testing "obstructs students' path to becoming lifelong, self-directed learners and alienates them from their own learning experiences in school" (2003, 33). See also Emery and Ohanian (2004).

9. Consider the absurdity of the NCLB requirement that all special education students will be proficient by 2014. Special education is a program for students whose academic performance is low; if they reach proficiency, they are likely to be moved out of the program. So it is literally impossible for

students in this category to reach proficiency. NCLB provisions regarding special education and English language learners were adjusted in 2004 and 2005, but this kind of tinkering does not cover over the law's disregard for educational and social realities. Consider also that approximately twenty-six thousand U.S. public schools—some of them long considered exemplary—have been stigmatized by NCLB and that some states (including Massachusetts, Connecticut, and Maine) are projecting AYP failure rates as high as 90 percent. See Goldberg (2005) and Neill et al. (2004).

10. Using four independent measures of student learning in high-stakes states, researchers Audrey Amrein and David Berliner (2003) found no increases and some declines. They did find decreased motivation among students and increases in early leaving (32). Similarly, Reeves (2002) has found that states with high-stakes assessment do not show higher student achievement than those without them. According to Reeves, the notion that consequences improve achievement is a myth.

11. Thomas Sowell (2003) is especially vicious in his attacks on "the education establishment," complaining, for instance, about "unionized incompetents" and "unbelievably dreary and stupid" education courses. As I write, details continue to come to light about the Bush administration's payoffs to Armstrong Williams in return for positive coverage of No Child Left Behind. See Hamburger and Wallsten (2005); "Syndicator Drops Writer" (2005); Will (2005).

12. In 2002, only 24 percent of respondents gave the nation's schools an A or a B, but 71 percent of parents gave an A or a B to the school their oldest child attended. In 2003, those numbers were 26 percent and 68 percent and in 2004, 26 percent and 70 percent. See Rose and Gallup (2002, 2003, 2004).

13. Writers such as Diane Ravitch (1983, 2000) and E. D. Hirsch (1988) portray "progressive" teachers as obsessed with students' self-esteem rather than traditional academic subjects. They charge these permissive, "soft" teachers with ruining kids' minds and maligning their "traditionalist" counterparts. This despite the fact that progressive education—in the tradition of John Dewey—never has been and is not today the dominant approach to education in U.S. public schools; see Tyack (1974); Cremin (1961); Darling-Hammond (1997, 9); Gallagher (2002b); Hillocks (2002); Kohn (1999).

14. Appropriately enough, NCLB touts the importance of "highly qualified teachers," but its definition of that term hinges almost exclusively on content knowledge and not on teachers' understanding of learning, curriculum development, assessment, collaboration, or reflective practice (see Chapter 5).

Teachers at the Lead, Schools in the Center

The Nebraska Story

Commissioner's STARS Advisory Committee Meeting, Lincoln, Nebraska, January 14, 2005

Pacing the front of the meeting room—why did I agree to facilitate today?—I watch them file in: teachers, administrators, district curriculum and assessment directors, Nebraska Department of Education (NDE) staff, and staff developers. The STARS Advisory Committee: the rudder of the state's School-based Teacher-led Assessment and Reporting System. As they stamp their feet and shake off the snow and bitter cold, I try to gauge their collective mood: Crabby? Happy to be inside? Ready to work? What do they think of the theme for today's meeting: *STARS After Five Years: Looking Back, Looking Ahead?* I catch few hints as they pour themselves coffee, nod and smile blandly to each other, and find their ways to open seats.

I turn to the whiteboard and write:

Effective leaders tolerate enough ambiguity to keep the creative juices flowing, but along the way (once they and the group know enough), they seek coherence.

Deep and sustained reform depends on many of us, not just on the very few who are destined to be extraordinary.

Michael Fullan [2001, 8–9, 2]

Turning back to the group, twenty-five strong now, I watch them squinting at my chicken-scratch handwriting. I begin by telling them why the Nebraska Department of Education has asked me to facilitate today. STARS is five years old now; our evaluation team has issued three annual reports. We know a lot about what is working and what is not in Nebraska's unique experiment in teacher-led, school-based school improvement. It's time to step outside the day-to-day work of "managing change," as Fullan might say, in order to reflect on it and shape it. My job as facilitator is to create the kind of space Fullan describes. I want us to try out new ideas, ask hard questions, wonder together—court ambiguity. And let's use the messiness we create to wend our way toward coherence, toward a reinvigorated sense of purpose for STARS.

They look game. I press on, ask them to consider Fullan's second quotation. Nowhere, I suggest, does "deep and sustained reform" depend more upon the many, rather than the few, than in Nebraska. Unlike other states, Nebraska has chosen to put teachers at the lead and schools in the center. STARS lives and dies by the many. And so we must remember today that each of us represents thousands of Nebraska teachers, school administrators, staff developers, students, parents, and community members.

Still game—still, at least, attentive. Time to write. I ask two questions: (1) What is the best thing about STARS as it has unfolded over the past five years? and (2) What is your biggest worry as STARS continues to develop?

Despite the early hour and the unhappy weather, fierce scribbling ensues.

We go around the room, share our responses. We fill sheet after sheet of chart paper. The testimony is powerful, the ideas rich. Good, productive chaos.

And then, once everyone has shared, we move toward coherence: What themes do we see? First, what do we value about STARS? The group decides STARS

♦ *sponsors connections:* it fosters collaboration, conversation, integration, articulation; educators—teachers and administrators—are talking and working (often for the first time) across subject areas and grades;

♦ *promotes teacher involvement and professional growth:* it is a teacher-led system, something teachers do, rather than something done to them; it provides teachers with motivation and support to stand back from their practice, reflect on it, and, where appropriate, change it;

♦ *is student-focused:* the system generates information that helps educators improve instruction and be more responsive to how each student learns;

♦ *encourages reflective, classroom-based assessment:* it puts assessment where it belongs: in the hands of classroom teachers, who use it as part of instruction;

♦ *is inclusive:* it involves (or strives to involve) all teachers, all students, all educational partners;

♦ *is a validation of the teaching profession:* it honors and trusts teachers' professional judgment, not only that of remote "experts"; and

♦ *inspires ownership and pride among Nebraska educators,* who value the state's choice to build its own, unique system, rather than patch together a system from the vagaries of external mandates.

That ownership, that pride, is palpable in the room. I want to linger here to savor the good energy in the room. I want to talk about what I have seen in other states, how strange it is to hear educators use these words—*connections, professional growth, validation, pride*—to describe a state assessment and reporting system. But time is running short and I promised time for hard questions and worries.

And so—with just as much chaotic enthusiasm and on just as many pieces of chart paper—we share, listen for threads, identify themes. The group generates a list of difficult questions: How can teachers handle—and find time for—the demands of the system, on top of the work they already do? How can we help community members better understand STARS? Will funding keep pace with the rising demands of the system and be sufficient to ensure high-quality professional development? How can we encourage our colleagues to choose being good over looking good? How do we address the inevitable credibility challenges to STARS in an era of standardized state tests? How do we involve all teachers in STARS, not just a few "stars"?

Clearly, STARS is neither perfect nor painless, and it faces serious challenges. I tell them it is time to roll up our sleeves. We will break into groups to discuss what schools, districts, and the state can do to protect and enhance the best features of STARS and to ameliorate or avoid the dangers and problems we've identified.

"But before we do that," I say, "I need a reality check. Does anyone in the room worry that STARS is not the right thing to do?"

As any teacher knows, there is silence—a quietness underneath which one can hear tiny nonsilences: the shuffling of feet, the tapping of pens, the soft clearing of throats—and then there is *silence.* Waiting out the half minute I believe my question deserves, I glance toward the half-frosted windows and almost convince myself that I can hear snow falling on snow.

<hr>

The members of the STARS Advisory Committee are like many of their colleagues around the country: unassuming, hardworking, committed to making the best decisions for their schools, communities, and kids. They don't consider themselves radicals, progressives, or even particularly political. They're just trying to do the right thing.

And yet, they find themselves at the center of considerable interest and controversy. The system they helped create, STARS, has been the subject of vitriolic attacks by the *Education Gadfly*, an online publication of the conservative Thomas B. Fordham Foundation (Porter-Magee 2004; Finn 2004; Christensen 2004). It has been slammed by *Education Week* in its annual reviews of state assessment and accountability for not having standardized tests and centralized authority (Editorial Projects in Education 1999–2005). It has been the focus of a special issue of *Educational Measurement: Issues and Practice* (June 2004) and articles in *Phi Delta Kappan* (Gallagher 2000; Gallagher 2004b; Roschewski 2003; Roschewski with Gallagher and Isernhagen 2001), *School Administrator* (Christensen 2001a; Joel 2001), and the *Chicago Tribune* (Dell'Angela 2004). It has been praised by the National Center for Fair and Open Testing (FairTest) as a model "authentic" state system that "provides valuable lessons for using assessment and accountability constructively" (Neill et al. 2004, 156). And it is the focus of an annual national conference devoted to classroom-based assessment.[1]

Interestingly, STARS is scorned by some and lauded by others for precisely the same reasons. It refuses high-stakes state tests in favor of district responsibility for designing and implementing assessments to measure student learning on standards. And it refuses direct comparisons between and rankings of schools and districts in favor of an improvement model that emphasizes schools' and districts' growth. Given the power of the accountability agenda, it's no wonder Nebraska has generated so much heat.

This chapter presents what I'm calling the Nebraska Story. I should note, though, that no one narrative could ever capture the complexity of Nebraskans' experiences. My choice of article notwithstanding, clearly I am telling *a* Nebraska story. It is a *true* story, to be sure, but other, equally true stories might be told as well. Because my purpose in this book is not to capture all the nuances of what is happening in Nebraska, but instead to offer teachers usable insights and practices, I feel free—indeed, I feel bound—to highlight the best of what is happening in the state. I will discuss from time to time the problems and limitations our research has uncovered—after all, the perils of this story are as instructive as its promise—but this book is not intended to be a research report; for that, I direct readers to the annual studies of the Comprehensive Evaluation Project, available at www.nde.state.ne.us/stars. In the meantime, I invite you to listen to and learn from *this* story: the one I believe teachers most need to hear.

The Setting

Nebraska is a study in contrasts. Although it is a largely rural state, nearly half of Nebraska's 1.7 million residents live in its two largest cities, Lincoln and Omaha. Although the state has relatively low racial diversity, its Latino population is exploding (thanks largely to the meatpacking industry) and the capital, Lincoln, is among the top twenty destination cities in the United States for newly arrived immigrants (Pipher 2002, 6). Although the state is an innovator in rural community development and renewal, its rural areas face crippling poverty and steady out-migration; in fact, Nebraska has the three poorest counties in the nation (Funk and Bailey 2000).

The state's politics are no less complex. Generally speaking, Nebraska is solidly Republican and socially conservative. But it shares with other Midwestern states a historically rooted aversion to big business—think of farmers' alliances against railroad companies in the late nineteenth century—and an affinity for grassroots politics and populist leaders like Williams Jennings Bryan and George Norris (Nye 1951). These traditional commitments have led to strange political anomalies like Nebraska's unicameral legislature, the only one of its kind in the country. As well, they have led the state to rebel against the conservative Bush administration's top-down approach to educational accountability, earning Nebraska the time-honored Midwestern honorific *maverick.*

Nebraska's resistance to the top-down approach of No Child Left Behind, then, is not shaped by a run-of-the-mill states' rights argument. Instead, it stems from Nebraskans' belief that schooling is a community responsibility. Indeed, Nebraskans have a special relationship to their public schools. This is especially so in many small towns, where the school is the community center. In the smallest rural towns, people know that if they lose their school, they lose the lifeblood of their community (Center for Rural Affairs Committee on Education 2000). But even in larger communities, citizens understand the importance of public education in this state where many business leaders, community VIPs, and elected officials are products of the state's public school system.

Nebraskans tend to support public education for another reason as well: Nebraska students are generally high achievers, consistently scoring above the national average on standardized tests such as the Metropolitan Achievement Test and the National Assessment of Educational Progress. These results, regularly touted in newspapers across the state, promote generally warm public regard for the state's schools and teachers.

At the same time, Nebraska educators face daunting challenges, including the loss of many smaller schools to consolidations, unifications, and closings. The number of districts in Nebraska has dwindled by approximately 20 percent in just the past few years; with the dissolution of some two hundred Class I (elementary-only) districts under way as I write, that percentage will grow to about 50 percent. At the same time, schools are adjusting to rapidly changing student demographics. As noted earlier, the Latino population is growing quickly, and for the first time, Nebraska districts are serving majority Spanish-speaking populations.

This is the complex setting of the Nebraska Story, the context in which the state's School-based, Teacher-led Assessment and Reporting System was conceived and implemented.

Laying the Groundwork

In the mid-1990s, Nebraska education itself was a study in contrasts. The state's students, on the whole, achieved well according to standard educational measures—but others were (as we now say) being left behind. Most Nebraska teachers were well qualified and doing wonderful work—but often in isolation and typically without the means or the expertise to gather reliable information on the effects of their practices on student learning. Many schools were the heart and soul of their communities, as they always had been—but some barely communicated with their constituents. In short, while public education in Nebraska was generally effective, some teachers, schools, and students were falling through the cracks.

Like their counterparts in other states at this time, Nebraska's new commissioner of education, Doug Christensen, and his Department of Education staff realized the state had not done enough to ensure that *all* students were well served by the public education system. So began the process of designing state standards and statewide assessment.

To this point, the Nebraska Story sounds like the story of any other state (though, as the forty-ninth state to adopt a standards, assessment, and accountability system, we might say it came a bit late to statewide reform). And in fact, Nebraska's legislatively mandated "measurable academic content standards" in reading, writing, math, science, social studies, and history do not look much different from those in other states. The development of the standards involved teachers from around Nebraska (Roschewski 2003), but it was largely a state-driven process. In this sense, Nebraska is not immune from the charges of critics who claim that standards are likely to promote a one-size-fits-all mentality, bureaucratic rigidity, and atomistic, narrow, or watered-down (a mile wide and an inch deep) curricula (Ohanian 2000; Emery and Ohanian 2004).

Here, though, the Nebraska Story takes a turn. And in this turning, we find a state attempting to drive a wedge between standards and standardization, between standard *guided* and standard *driven*, between focus and rigidity, between commitment and compliance. First, in Nebraska, districts are required to adopt standards that are "the same as, equal to, or exceeding" the state-designed standards. And so many Nebraska districts have designed their own standards, typically with a level and quality of teacher involvement that no state could achieve. Although the Nebraska Department of Education approves local standards, the districts that have gone through this process have found it to be a valuable tool for building shared local commitment to articulated goals.

But the most profound turn in The Nebraska Story—the one that makes it unlike that of any other state in the country—involves assessment: the preferred tool (read: weapon) of the accountability agenda. (Without assessment, standards are mere statements; with it, they take on enormous power.) While other states opted for high-stakes state tests to measure student learning on standards, Nebraska chose to develop a *statewide system of local assessments*, which allows individual districts to design their own assessment systems. It did so not only because a centralized system would be anathema to this staunchly local-control state but also because, as Commissioner Christensen (2001a) put it, "much of the power of assessment is lost when it is not integrated into classroom activities." This much was clear from the testing regimes in other states, which were spawning narrow curricula, emphasis on lower-order skills, decreased teacher and student engagement, and the other problems cataloged in Chapter 2. These trends inspired Nebraska to develop its school-based, teacher-led system (Roschewski 2004).

Despite Nebraska's tradition of local control of education, Christensen faced an uphill battle at a time when top-down, state-test-driven accountability reforms were sweeping the nation. Indeed, in 1998, the Nebraska legislature followed the lead of its cohorts around the country and mandated a single state test.

Before that legislation went into effect, however, Christensen and his colleagues at the Nebraska Department of Education lobbied hard for their vision. They marshaled the support of measurement experts who enumerated the problems with and limitations of standardized, high-stakes tests. They shared what was happening in other states. They documented the high quality of Nebraska's existing system. And in the end, they won the day. In the spring of 2000, the Nebraska legislature passed Legislative Bill 812, which paved the way for the implementation of Nebraska's STARS (Roschewski 2004, 9–10).

Getting STARS off the Ground

The challenges of implementing a school-based, teacher-led system are obvious. How could the state ensure the reliability and validity of a system that had hundreds of local assessment programs in operation at the same time? How could it handle the huge volume of documentation that would be required? How could it ensure that teachers were well trained, especially in the area of assessment—not exactly a staple of traditional teacher preparation and professional development? And perhaps most dauntingly, how could it mobilize local educators to take on a set of responsibilities they were likely—especially considering Nebraskans' don't-tread-on-me ideology—to view with a jaundiced eye?

As one would expect, Nebraska policymakers and educators continue to struggle with these challenges, even five years after the implementation of STARS. But the policies, procedures, and practices they have developed must be understood within the context of a larger set of principles that have shaped the system.

Nebraska's approach to systemic school reform—Nebraskans prefer the term *school improvement*—is radically different from that of the accountability agenda I described in Chapter 2. In fact, we might say it turns the accountability agenda inside out. Its central premise is that meaningful, sustainable school improvement is possible only by empowering schools to build their capacity, not by attempting to control them from outside. So instead of leveraging compliance with incentives and disincentives, the system is designed to promote local capacity building for school improvement.

A key premise here is that assessment is an instructional tool, not a policy tool. Instead of building an assessment instrument that puts schools in competition with one another—a state test that ranks schools—Nebraska has asked its districts to build assessment instruments that will help them compete with *themselves*: that is, to improve over time. This approach to assessment removes the incentive for the kinds of underhanded score-boosting tactics we saw in Chapter 2, allowing educators instead to use what they learn from assessment to develop effective teaching and learning for all students. They also use assessment results to inform other educational partners—primarily parents but also other community members—and to engage them in probing, well-informed conversations about how best to support and enhance student learning.

Ultimately, STARS aims to effect a sea change in school cultures across the state. Like many educational researchers and observers, Nebraskans recognize that while outside reformers can *change* schools—can restructure them, for instance—only those within schools can truly *improve* them (see, for instance, Barth 2001; Deal and Peterson 1999; Fullan 1993; Hargreaves 1995; Huffman and Hipp 2003; Westheimer 1998). Refusing the premise of No Child Left Behind that only some schools are in need of improvement, STARS asks all schools to improve—from within.

Here's how STARS works. Each district in Nebraska is responsible for developing its own assessment process, though many do so in collaboration with other districts or with regional education service units. The expectation is that these assessment processes will be integrated up and down grade levels and across content areas. Indeed, the Nebraska Department of Education encourages and provides assistance to all districts to develop K–12 approaches to curriculum and assessment that allow them to track individual students' development. However, annual *reporting* to the state—conceived as only one piece of a fuller, locally meaningful process—is confined to three "guidepost" grades (4, 8, and 11) and core content areas (reading, writing, math, and soon science and social studies).

Districts measure student learning on standards in various ways. Some develop districtwide criterion-referenced tests. Others rely heavily on classroom assessments. Still others devise some combination of these. Most incorporate some norm-referenced tests to cover a handful of standards, though only 30 to 35 percent of Nebraska standards are addressed by widely available standardized tests (Christensen 2001a). In any case, districts are encouraged to develop assessments that suit their curricular and instructional goals. Nebraska asks all its districts and schools to meet the same learning standards, but *how* they do so varies widely.

However, districts are required to document not only their students' performance but also the quality of the assessments used to measure that performance. At present, the reporting mechanism is called a District Assessment Portfolio (DAP). DAPs are sent each year to the Nebraska Department of Education, where they are evaluated by local and national assessment experts. Districts receive two ratings on their DAPs: one for student performance and one for assessment quality.

The student performance side is relatively straightforward: districts report the percentage of students who meet each standard. The assessment quality documentation includes a description of the assessment process, an explanation of how those assessments meet state-designed Quality Criteria (QC), and samples of those assessments. The six QC (see Figure 3–1) are intended to ensure technical quality, but they are also hallmarks of good assessment practice.

The DAP, at least in its current form, soon will be a thing of the past. One of the ideas that emerged from the STARS Advisory Committee meeting depicted earlier was regular, on-site visits to districts to provide both summative and formative feedback not only on technical assessment quality but also on what is *done* with assessment data: how it feeds back into instruction and assessment. The details of this process are still being worked out as I write, but one of its attractions is that it still allows expert review of assessment quality (as required by Nebraska statute) while providing Nebraska educators more detailed and useful feedback about assessment as part of school improvement. (A side benefit is the involvement of Nebraska educators in the team visits: a validation of their professional growth.)

Whatever form state reporting and feedback take, the architects of STARS are committed to using multiple measures of student performance. In addition to locally designed assessments, the system includes a statewide writing assessment (SWA) and regular reporting of students' scores on national standardized tests (separate from reporting

Nebraska's Six Quality Criteria

1. Assessments align to state or local standards.

2. Students have an opportunity to learn the content.

3. Assessments are free from bias or offensive language.

4. The level is developmentally age appropriate for students.

5. There is consistency in scoring.

6. The mastery levels are appropriate to subject and grade level.

Figure 3–1 Nebraska's Six Quality Criteria

on standards). The SWA, like many such tests around the country, requires students to produce an essay on an assigned prompt in a timed environment. Writing experts—myself included—have criticized on-demand writing tests for (among other things) promoting formulaic writing and severely constricting students' (and teachers') conceptions of the writing process.[2] But in the eyes of many observers, the SWA lends legitimacy to this otherwise locally controlled system (indeed, it was added to the system as a political sop to legislative opponents of the local approach). In any case, the SWA initially rotated among grades 4, 8, and 11. Beginning in 2003–4, it was included as an "academic indicator" for Adequate Yearly Progress (AYP) under No Child Left Behind (NCLB) requirements and is now conducted annually in all three grades.

This shift in the SWA schedule shows one way in which the provisions of NCLB have been integrated into STARS. (Like every other state, Nebraska has not been fully approved under NCLB; it currently operates under the Elementary and Secondary Education Act.) Many Nebraska schools do not have the minimum number of students in demographic categories to be reported under AYP provisions, but for those who do, STARS data are used to monitor AYP. Because STARS remains the primary assessment system in the state, only grades 4, 8, and 11 are assessed and reported by standard. However, under AYP, districts must report progress in reading and math for grades 3, 5, 6, and 7, as well as one high school grade. The state has worked with districts to identify one focus area for each subject (comprehension in reading, for instance). In keeping with Nebraska's local approach, districts determine how to measure this progress (by classroom assessments, district-designed assessments, or national tests). Most schools were already assessing at these grade levels. In any event, AYP is determined using a combination of student performance and participation rates in assessments, the SWA, graduation rates, and district assessment quality.

Along with demographic information and other key information about each school, state reporting data are compiled in the annual *State of the Schools Report*. This report—available online in English and Spanish at the Nebraska Department of Education website (www.nde.state.ne.us)—allows readers to access school, district, and state results. Information from it is abstracted for an annual state report card, which is disseminated in newspapers across the state.

In addition to public reporting, STARS includes other accountability provisions. In order to meet state accountability goals, districts must earn ratings of exemplary, very good, or good (the other ratings are needs improvement and unacceptable) in both assessment quality and student performance. If they do not, they receive assistance from the Nebraska Department of Education and their regional educational service unit. According to state board policy, they have one year to raise their assessment quality rating and three years to raise their student performance rating or they are in violation of Nebraska's Accreditation Rule and risk losing accreditation.

When we compare these provisions with the draconian consequences we see in other states—negative sanctions in Kentucky's system, for instance, include academic audits, state intervention, probation, hiring and firing of principals and teachers, and revocation of teacher tenure (Foster 2000)—it becomes clear that STARS is built on facilitative, not punitive, policy. Commissioner Christensen and his staff view their primary purpose not as wielding carrots and sticks but as supporting the schools and helping them build capacity to improve. They conduct countless school visits, provide hands-on assistance to schools and districts struggling with assessment tasks, disseminate clear, easy-to-read updates on STARS, offer portfolio workshops for formative feedback, provide professional development workshops, meetings, and trainings—the list goes on. Clearly, Nebraska policymakers devote the bulk of their resources not to designing controls—to invoke Linda Darling-Hammond's (1997) useful distinction—but to building capacity.

Charting STARS: Early Results

In Chapter 1, I claimed that the measure of an idea is its fruit, its consequences. Because STARS represents a novel idea, a unique theory of school improvement, we must examine what it *does* and what it *renders*. How is it making a difference in Nebraska schools and communities? In the remainder of this chapter, I begin to answer this question by presenting some statewide results from the first few years after the implementation of STARS. To be sure, STARS is still a young system and these data must be considered preliminary. My purpose here is to paint the Nebraska Story in broad strokes, and so I focus briefly on three questions: (1) How has student performance changed under STARS? (2) How has assessment quality changed under STARS? and (3) How have school cultures changed under STARS? (Readers interested in learning more about the results referenced here are invited to consult the annual reports of the

Comprehensive Evaluation Project: Gallagher 2002a, 2003, 2004a; Isernhagen 2005.) The portrait I begin to sketch here will become more detailed in later chapters, as I explore what teachers can learn from the Nebraska Story.

Student Performance Results

Without getting overly technical, there are a number of things to keep in mind as we look at statewide student performance results. First, we are examining different groups (fourth, eighth, and eleventh grade) of students each year. Second, when districts report to the state the percentage of students who are proficient on standards, they use their own assessments and cut scores (though according to Quality Criterion 6, they must provide evidence that they are using an appropriate process for establishing those cut scores). Third, the state uses another set of cut scores to rate each district's student performance as exemplary, very good, good, needs improvement, or unacceptable. If 79 percent of a district's students are proficient on math standards, for instance, is that exemplary, very good, and so forth? The state must establish ranges of scores to determine appropriate ratings. (These ranges are established through a process led by the Buros Center for Testing and includes educators from across the state.[3]) Finally, remember that in order to meet state accountability goals, districts must receive one of the top three ratings on student performance.

The chart in Figure 3–2 shows the percentages of districts earning each of the student performance ratings for the first five years under STARS. (Note that districts reported on both mathematics and reading in 2004–5.) One can see even at a glance that as time passes, more districts are earning exemplary ratings and fewer are falling into the lower ratings. As well, we see marked improvement when we examine the data by content area. For instance, in 2001–2, 45 percent of districts earned an exemplary student performance rating in mathematics for fourth grade. In the next round of math reporting, 2003–4, that percentage was up to 71 percent. In the most recent round, 2004–5, that number has climbed even further, to 79 percent. This upward trend is the same at all three grade levels and in both content areas (though it is most pronounced in fourth grade). Perhaps the best news in these data for Nebraska school districts is that by 2004–5, very few of them failed to meet state accountability requirements by falling into the bottom two categories.

Statisticians and psychometricians are hard at work analyzing and developing new metrics to explore Nebraska's unconventional data

Percentage of Nebraska School Districts by Student Performance Rating

Grade 4	2000–2001 Reading	2001–2 Math	2002–3 Reading	2003–4 Math	2004–5 Reading	2004–5 Math
Exemplary	31.8%	45.4%	42.7%	70.6%	66.1%	79.1%
Very Good	39.8%	27.2%	38.9%	16.7%	23.3%	12.9%
Good	18.9%	19.4%	14.3%	8.7%	7.9%	5.5%
Needs Improvement	5.0%	5.5%	2.6%	2.4%	1.7%	1.7%
Unacceptable	4.6%	2.5%	1.4%	1.7%	.8%	1.0%

Grade 8	2000–2001 Reading	2001–2 Math	2002–3 Reading	2003–4 Math	2004–5 Reading	2004–5 Math
Exemplary	34.1%	30.3%	35.2%	41.2%	59.2%	59.1%
Very Good	34.4%	27.6%	44.9%	30.5%	33.3.%	25.7%
Good	22.4%	32.2%	15.8%	23.8%	4.8%	11.9%
Needs Improvement	7.8%	7.1%	3.3%	3.4%	1.5%	1.5%
Unacceptable	1.4%	2.8%	.8%	1.1%	1.8%	1.8%

Grade 11	2000–2001 Reading	2001–2 Math	2002–3 Reading	2003–4 Math	2004–5 Reading	2004–5 Math
Exemplary	23.6%	18.3%	21.5%	30%	47.9%	41.3%
Very Good	48.7%	26.2%	53.6%	29.2%	40.1%	36.6%
Good	18.7%	39.5%	22.2%	35.8%	11.3%	17.1%
Needs Improvement	8.6%	14.1%	2.3%	4.2%	.8%	5.1%
Unacceptable	.4%	1.9%	.4%	.8%	0%	0%

Data from Nebraska Department of Education

Figure 3–2 Percentage of Nebraska School Districts by Student Performance Rating

(Brookhart 2003, 2005; Buckendahl, Plake, and Impara 2004; Plake, Impara, and Buckendahl 2004). However, we do know, based on studies conducted by independent researchers, that while students' performance on their districts' assessments have risen steadily in both content areas at all three grade levels, their performance on national, normed tests has remained steady or increased slightly (Gallagher 2004a; Isernhagen 2005). This is important because districts' emphasis on their own assessment is not having a detrimental impact on students' performance on tests designed to measure Nebraska students' academic achievement relative to that of their national peers (Isernhagen 2005, 124).

Another measure of Nebraska students' academic performance is the Statewide Writing Assessment, which, as I noted previously, ini-

Percentage of Students Proficient on Statewide Writing Assessment				
	2001–2	2002–3	2003–4	2004–5
Grade 4	73%		80%	83%
Grade 8		75%	83%	85%
Grade 11			87%	90%
Data from Nebraska Department of Education				

Figure 3–3 *Percentage of Students Proficient on Statewide Writing Assessment*

tially rotated among grades 4, 8, and 11, but beginning in 2003–4, is now administered annually in all three grades (see Figure 3–3). Although we have only two years of multigrade testing, the results of the SWA are encouraging; a higher percentage of students each year at each grade level have attained proficiency in writing.

Of course, the CEP will continue to examine trend data as they become available, and we will conduct more sophisticated analyses. But for now, these steady increases in student performance on these disparate measures can only be read as positive signs.

Assessment Quality Results

Recall that District Assessment Portfolios are evaluated for assessment quality against six Quality Criteria: (1) match to standards, (2) opportunity to learn, (3) freedom from bias, (4) developmental appropriateness, (5) scoring consistency, and (6) appropriate mastery levels. The reviewers—nationally recognized assessment experts paired with credentialed Nebraska educators (who help formulate feedback to districts)—are trained by the Buros Center for Testing, a well-respected measurement organization that has consulted with the Nebraska Department of Education from the beginning of STARS. Using a common rubric, reviewers are asked to rate assessment quality as exemplary, very good, good, needs improvement, or unacceptable.

The chart in Figure 3–4 is designed to display the same kind of data as Figure 3–2, but this time, the results reflect the percentages of districts earning each of the ratings for assessment quality. Again, one can examine the chart year by year and see that the percentages in the higher categories increase while the percentages in the lower categories decrease. This holds true as well when we isolate each content area; if we examine grade 8 reading, for instance, we see that in the first round of reporting (2000–2001), only 13 percent of districts received an exemplary rating, while 34 percent failed to meet state accountability goals by falling into one of the lower two categories. By the second round (2002–3), 53 percent were rated exemplary and only 6 percent fell into the bottom two categories. In the most recent round (2004–5), 56 percent were rated exemplary and 0 percent were rated needs improvement or unacceptable.

We would expect portfolio ratings to increase during the first few years after implementation; district personnel are learning how to put together an effective DAP, just as students learn to become better at taking certain kinds of tests after repeated experiences with them. At the same time, the consistently strong improvement across five years provides evidence that Nebraska districts' assessment processes are sound. Moreover, a recent independent evaluation of local district assessments by classroom assessment expert Susan Brookhart found

Percentage of Districts by Assessment Quality Ratings						
Grade 4	**2000–2001 Reading**	**2001–2 Math**	**2002–3 Reading**	**2003–4 Math**	**2004–5 Reading**	**2004–5 Math**
Exemplary	15.6%	30.2%	49.0%	68.2%	52.3%	68.8%
Very Good	46.3%	46.5%	40.7%	29.7%	45.0%	30.1%
Good	4.4%	6.6%	1.1%	.7%	.5%	.7%
Needs Improvement	25.6%	8.5%	2.1%	.7%	0%	.5%
Unacceptable	8.2%	8.2%	7.1%	.7%	2.3%	0%
Grade 8	**2000–2001 Reading**	**2001–2 Math**	**2002–3 Reading**	**2003–4 Math**	**2004–5 Reading**	**2004–5 Math**
Exemplary	13.5%	32.3%	53%	81.5%	56.4%	80.5%
Very Good	48.5%	43.9%	39.6%	17.1%	43.1%	19%
Good	3.8%	6.5%	1.1%	.3%	.3%	.3%
Needs Improvement	25.3%	8.9%	1.9%	.6%	0%	.3%
Unacceptable	8.9%	8.4%	4.5%	.6%	.3%	0%
Grade 11	**2000–2001 Reading**	**2001–2 Math**	**2002–3 Reading**	**2003–4 Math**	**2004–5 Reading**	**2004–5 Math**
Exemplary	16.6%	33.3%	51.3%	83.9%	54.5%	84.1%
Very Good	47.6%	44.3%	41%	15%	45.1%	15.1%
Good	4.1%	6.4%	.4%	.4%	.4%	.4%
Needs Improvement	21.8%	9.9%	3.1%	.4%	0%	.4%
Unacceptable	10%	6.1%	4.2%	.4%	0%	0%

Data from Nebraska Department of Education

Figure 3–4 Percentage of Districts by Assessment Quality Ratings

that the overall quality of mathematics assessments was good (2005, 14). And finally, as we will see, the qualitative data collected by the Comprehensive Evaluation Project reveal enormous growth among teachers and administrators across the state in what Nebraska educators call "assessment literacy." So while we should read the data with a grain of salt, we have every reason to believe the story they seem to tell: that assessment quality in Nebraska is strong overall and getting stronger.

Changes in School Cultures

While numerical data like those I've shared do tell an important story, we must remember that learning and assessment performance are not the same thing. In fact, as Alfie Kohn suggests, single-minded pursuit of "levels of achievement" can blind educators and students to "layers of learning" (1999, 27). With this caveat in mind, the researchers associated with the Comprehensive Evaluation Project have concentrated the bulk of our energies on learning what was happening in the field. If the animating idea of STARS is that only those within schools can truly improve them, then it is necessary to examine how (or whether) school cultures are changing in Nebraska.

Accordingly, in addition to conducting several large surveys of educators, CEP researchers have spent hundreds of hours in schools. In the three years from which I draw most of the qualitative data for this book, 2002–4, we conducted approximately 350 interviews in seventy-three schools located in thirty Nebraska districts. We visited some of these schools annually; others were included in the study for only one or two years. Our school sample was representative according to geography (regions within the state), school and community size (including urban, rural, and suburban), student demographics (by poverty, race, language), and student and school achievement results.[4]

Even in the relatively short span of three years, we observed decided shifts in the cultures of Nebraska schools. Indeed, STARS has prompted a radical change in the way many educators understand and go about their work. Here, I summarize only three overarching themes our researchers identified; these themes, and more specific ones as well, will be explored in subsequent chapters.

Developing Teacher Leadership

Perhaps the most marked shift in Nebraska schools under STARS has been the flourishing of teacher leadership. Teacher-leaders in Nebraska play different roles and hold different positions. They may be school or district assessment coordinators and wield strong authority by virtue of administrative cachet. Or they may exert their leadership in more subtle ways—by convincing colleagues to try student-led parent conferences, serving on a school improvement task force, writing for the local newspaper, organizing an after-school writing club, participating in the rotating facilitation of a curriculum committee, and so on. Teacher leadership in Nebraska schools is a practice, not a position, condition, or achievement. And at the heart of this practice is the building of meaningful, reciprocal relationships not only with students but also with educational partners outside the classroom, including colleagues, parents, and other community members.

Examples of teacher leadership abound in our research. An amusing one comes from a small K–12 school. During an interview, a third-grade teacher related the following story:

> The other day we felt really bad because we called a [curriculum and assessment] meeting and we put it at the bottom of the bulletin board. But nobody had . . . told [our principal]. So we had the meeting after school and it happened to be in my room. The teachers from the high school came down. [The principal] came in right as we were finishing. He said, "Nobody invited me."

Whatever sympathy we mustered for the principal, however, vanished when we interviewed him. He told us the same story, but with a very different moral:

> Two weeks ago they had a curriculum and assessment meeting and I wasn't even invited. And it was great. I mean, it was awesome in that they have now assumed so much of the control and responsibility for that that they feel comfortable without having me.

This twice-told tale, while unique, speaks to a larger trend across the three years of our study: teachers taking increased responsibility for instruction, curriculum, and assessment. Because many Nebraska teachers are coming to see these activities as intertwined, they see each as part of their job. Gone are the days when administrators handed them curriculum and assessments (usually in the form of textbooks); teachers are involved now in developing curriculum and designing assessments. And because instruction, curriculum, and assessment all fall under the umbrella of school improvement, teachers are becoming the leaders of school improvement in their buildings and districts.

Creating Collaborative Cultures

One of the most interesting, and perhaps surprising, shifts in Nebraska schools' cultures is the steady movement toward collaboration: among teachers, between teachers and administrators, and also (though to a lesser extent) between educators and parents and other community members. When we began visiting schools, many teachers, perhaps even the majority, clung to their traditional autonomy and resisted what they saw as the state's encroachment on their professional purview (the closed-door classroom). This is hardly surprising in a local-control state and given how outsiders—administrators, policymakers, politicians, pundits, the media—have used assessment as a tool of surveillance in a high-stakes game of gotcha. But over time, Nebraska teachers have come to see assessment as an *instructional* tool. And they have come to see that protectionism leads to isolation, which leads to professional stagnation (Elmore 2004). Today, the majority of Nebraska teachers believe their schools and students can succeed only if teachers come out of their classrooms and work together with their colleagues and other educational partners. This belief is so strong that the term *teacher in private practice* has become an epithet among many Nebraska teachers.

The dispositional shift I'm describing has not been sudden or complete. It might best be described as a form of *erosion*: Little by little, in most schools, teachers are giving up their role as jealous patrollers of the borders of their classrooms. And little by little, they are coming to take collective ownership of school improvement, including instruction, curriculum, and assessment. Clearly, it takes time to develop trust in one another and in the processes they are building. But in most schools, that is happening and teachers are working together not only within the content areas and grade levels but also across them. The following testimony comes from a teacher and assessment coordinator in a midsize district in the eastern part of the state, but it could have been culled from almost any of our study schools:

> You see teachers having more conversation about curriculum and instruction and assessment than ever before—and I have been a teacher for a number of years. . . . [Before, e]verybody did their own little thing: you know, you went in your room and you did it any way you chose as long as you covered basic things. And now teachers are working together, which to me is more equitable for kids.

This is as articulate a rendering of the cultural shift I'm describing as we could hope to find. Although the schools we visited were at different stages in creating collaborative cultures, they were all, in one way or another, developing common goals and a common language through regular, collegial dialogue.

Committing to Continuous Improvement, Constant Learning

That dialogue typically centers on one thing: school improvement. But perhaps it is misleading to say so, because, again, school improvement is an umbrella concept for a wide range of activities, including curriculum, instruction, assessment, professional development, and public engagement. And this is the point: school improvement has become the engine that drives and coordinates the various activities of many of the schools in our study.

Something extremely powerful happens for teachers when they lead the school improvement charge: They see how the various things they do in their school come together into an intentional, coherent whole. Each teacher in such a system understands how his or her work contributes to the school's overall effort to improve student learning. Each teacher helps shape that effort and feels like a valuable part of it. And each teacher understands that in order to sustain the process, they must ground it not in the need to meet external mandates, but in the need to act on internal commitments.

Indeed, a shared commitment to creating a culture of continuous improvement creates a potent centripetal force. There is integrity to such a process when teacher-leaders guide it with the ever present question How will this help students learn? Here is how one superintendent explained the process his district has put in place:

> It's child centered. And as long as it remains child centered, we're going to be OK. It's not perfect. It's going to change. We know that. We expect that. We expect to improve every year…That's the expectation that we have for our kids; that's the expectation we have for ourselves. Every teacher here is expected to improve.

His teachers agreed. A high school language arts teacher explained that designing and implementing a local assessment system "made us have to contend with the whole concept of process." She acknowledged that some of her colleagues ask, "When are we going to be done with this?" Her response: "Never.…We're never going to be done with it because it is just the nature of the work. It is a process, and so that's the way it is."

Not every Nebraska school, much less teacher, has made this commitment. Some teachers insist that "this assessment stuff" has nothing to do with student learning. And in fact, considering how their districts are handling the responsibility to develop a local assessment system, they are sometimes right. In these districts, assessment and reporting remain mere compliance requirements—things to get done before getting back to the "real work" of teaching and learning. But each year, we visited a growing number of educators and schools whose educators were beginning to see local assessment as an opportunity to focus on continuous improvement and student learning.

Epilogue

As my depiction of the STARS Advisory Committee meeting at the beginning of this chapter suggests, Nebraska educators are proud of what has transpired in this state over the last five years—but also apprehensive about the prospects of their unique approach to school improvement. There is, first of all, ample reason for optimism: student performance is improving, assessment quality is rising, and in more and more schools, traditional school cultures of isolation, competition, and mutual distrust are giving way to cultures of teacher-led, collaborative, continuous improvement.

But STARS faces many challenges, as well. *Time* continues to be the most daunting challenge for teachers, and the state and its districts must continue to find ways to alleviate the burden on teachers and create reward systems that are commensurate with the considerable expansion of their professional responsibilities. Another challenge is limited teacher ownership. Despite the clear overall trends toward teacher leadership and teacher engagement, some teachers in each school remain out of the loop. This is especially true in nonreporting grades and nonreported subjects and in large schools and districts. A third challenge is endemic to a decentralized system: Not all districts and schools are making good choices about how to meet their responsibilities, especially with respect to assessment. The state must help struggling districts avoid the search for administrative quick fixes, like contracting out to take care of assessment, rather than building internal capacity. This links to yet another challenge: maintaining support for accessible, high-quality professional development, both for new teachers and for veteran teachers. This enormous task involves nurturing partnerships among institutions of higher education, regional educational service units and other service providers, districts, and the Nebraska Department of Education. Finally, if STARS is to be sustainable, its proponents will need to make the case for it at a time when educational "common sense" runs in the opposite direction. The NDE will need to win final approval from the federal government, of course, but community engagement and support within the state will be just as crucial.

For now, it is fair to say that there are many positive signs for STARS, but its long-range sustainability remains an open question. My belief is that STARS represents the next generation of school reform: a model for the twenty-first century. But even if it does not— indeed, even if it were to disappear tomorrow—this unprecedented experiment in school improvement provides valuable insights for teachers working in any context. It opens up new possibilities for thinking about assessment, school improvement, and accountability—and whose responsibility, in the final analysis, these ought to be.

Notes

1. Information about the Leadership for Classroom Assessment Conference may be found at www.lcaconference.com.

2. In addition to Gallagher (2002a), see Hillocks (2002).

3. Readers interested in the technical aspects of this process, or in the other Buros-led processes mentioned in this book, are invited to consult the technical reports located on the Buros website: www.unl.edu/buros.

4. The CEP's annual reports include descriptions of research protocols.

Engaging Students

Making Assessment Meaningful in the Classroom

You're attending an academic conference. A panel has just finished. Sitting in the audience, you are inspired by your colleagues' work and words; your head is abuzz with new ideas. As the conversation begins, you are caught up immediately in the potent energy of professional exchange: you are a teacher among teachers.

And then, seemingly inevitably, someone—maybe a panelist, maybe an audience member—turns the conversation on a dime. "This is all fine and good," this someone offers, "but what about assessment?"

And the air is sucked out of the room. People look like they literally cannot breathe. Some shake their heads in evident frustration; others form wry, sad smiles; the rest begin packing up to leave for the next session. A few people offer dry plaints: "I have no time for what I think the kids really need." "This isn't why I got into teaching." "We shouldn't let this happen." But enthusiasm wanes and the conversation sputters. And none too soon, it is time to break.

———◆———

I have come to think of this phenomenon-cum-ritual as a symptom of assessment despair. I wager most teachers (and even more ex-teachers) have fallen victim, at one time or another, to assessment despair. It grips them when they and their students are treated as little more than entries on a ledger, numbers to be crunched. Or when they feel powerless in the face of an anonymous bureaucracy. Or when they recognize with bracing clarity that they participate in the dehumanization of the kids they've vowed to teach.

Assessment despair is understandable. It is a natural response to the calculated assault by the accountability agenda on what should be most sacrosanct in education: the relationship between teacher and student. The accountability agenda takes what should be deeply humanizing experiences—teaching and learning—and turns them into bloodless exercises in quality control. It takes what should be the ennobling work of democratic life—learning to live well together—and turns it into the cultivation of human capital. And it has hijacked assessment for this purpose, turning it from an instructional tool into a policy tool. Assessment has become the surveillance device of choice for politicians, policymakers, and administrators charged with maintaining "an efficient and accountable bureaucracy" (Huot 2002, 1). And when high stakes are attached, it becomes a weapon wielded against teachers and students who don't measure up, who fall outside the normative, who aren't deemed to be repaying the investment made in them.

But however reasonable, assessment despair is the enemy of effective teaching and learning. It's the enemy of *engagement*. A despairing teacher cannot offer hope to students, and without hope—without the belief that *things could be better*—we have no need to inquire, imagine, wonder, explore, discover, or even to learn. No engaged and engaging relationship was ever built in the absence of hope.

Engaging Assessment

The Nebraska Story is a narrative of hope—the hope that teachers can reclaim assessment from its hijackers and refashion it as a tool of engagement. Good teachers know that's just what assessment is; they assess their students every day, honing their powers of observation and professional judgment. They know assessment is the feedback loop that connects teaching and learning: the mechanism by which they and students get information about the effects of their work together. They are not surprised at recent research demonstrating that high-quality classroom assessment promotes learning (Black and Wiliam 1998; Guskey 2003; Stiggins 2004b). No, for them, assessment has always been an instructional tool. And it would be impossible to build engaging classrooms without it.

Nebraska has refused to join the Holy Grail quest for the Perfect Test because it views *the teacher as the primary assessment instrument*. The thinking goes like this: If assessments are to promote learning, not just report on it, then the people involved in the learning—teachers and students—must determine how to gather, interpret, and act on good information about their work together. They are the primary stakeholders of that activity, not remote technicians, policymakers, or investors.

While inimical to the accountability agenda, this approach to assessment is in step with dramatic shifts in the field of educational assessment over the last two decades. In general, those shifts have centered on expanding the concept of validity to include not only traditional technical issues but also the *uses* to which assessments are put—their *consequences* (Huot 2002; Broad 2003; Cronbach 1990; Messick 1989; Moss 1992). In other words, while validity was once viewed as an intrinsic quality of an assessment instrument, it has come to encompass as well the decisions made in response to data collected from the instrument.[1]

And yet, considering the extent to which the accountability agenda has controlled the meaning and uses of assessment, the very idea that assessment can actually promote learning, rather than merely check for it, constitutes a "major breakthrough" (Stiggins 2004a, 22; see also Guskey 2003). STARS places Nebraska in the vanguard of next-generation assessment by returning assessment to the classroom and focusing on assessment *for* learning, not just assessment *of* learning (Stiggins 2004a, 2004b; see also Black and Wiliam 1998; Black et al. 2004).

Another way to frame Nebraska's approach to assessment is to say that it opts for "high impact" over "high stakes" (Gallagher 2004b). STARS includes no high-stakes assessments, if by that we mean state tests to which are attached drastic consequences for students (retention in grade, denial of graduation), educators (salary, job security), or schools (reconstitution, closing). While accountability hawks claim that states cannot leverage change without clear and consistent extrinsic incentives and disincentives, STARS hinges on the notion that assessments can have a strong impact without attaching high stakes. Indeed, in light of the overwhelming evidence of the corrupting influence of high stakes (see Chapter 2), Nebraskans believe that impact is far more likely to have positive effects on teaching and learning when assessment is in the hands of teachers than when it is controlled by a regulating body or a profiteering industry.

High-impact assessment is conducted on site, in real time, and is driven by instruction. It doesn't ignore the stakes of assessment, but it recognizes that the most important incentives are embedded in the work that teachers and students do together (Elmore 2004). High-impact assessment is a tool of *engagement* between teachers and students. Figure 4–1 demonstrates, once again, how an engagement perspective differs from, and in many ways reverses, the accountability agenda.

Two Views of Assessment	
Accountability	**Engagement**
Threat	Opportunity
Top-down	Bottom-up or inside-out
Policy tool	Instructional tool
High stakes	High impact
Standardized tests	Teacher-designed assessments
Assessment *OF* learning	Assessment *FOR* Learning
Assessment-driven instruction	Instruction-driven assessment
Event-based	Ongoing, embedded
Students subjected	Students involved

Figure 4–1 *Two Views of Assessment*

Assessment in Nebraska Schools

In Nebraska, teachers are responsible for assessment. By this, I don't mean that handfuls of carefully selected teachers (i.e., those likely to support the state's agenda) are gathered in the state capital to participate in the design of statewide tests. Rather, each *district's* teachers develop, administer, and respond to the results of student assessments. It's not unheard of in Nebraska for a district to replicate the familiar state model, cherry picking a small, cooperative cadre of teachers to design districtwide tests while the vast majority of teachers in the district remain outside the process. But few Nebraska districts have chosen this route (or are even big enough to do so); instead, many teachers across the state are intimately involved in their district's assessment process.

Districts use a range of assessments, from pencil-and-paper criterion-referenced tests to performance assessments, as suits the individual district. Most districts have incorporated classroom assessment into their district process, which means that assessment truly is in the hands of classroom teachers. The assessments used for state reporting—and of course not all of them fall into this category—must be reviewed for Nebraska's six Quality Criteria: alignment to standards, opportunity to learn, freedom from bias, developmental appropriateness, scoring consistency, and appropriateness of mastery levels. This review is typically conducted locally by qualified panels of educators.

While these criteria are for the most part simply good assessment practice, it's worth pausing here to acknowledge a limitation of STARS in its current form. The six QC are all technical features of assessments emerging from traditional psychometrics. It has been both educationally and politically advantageous for the state of Nebraska to engage the psychometric community and to partner with the renowned Buros Institute. After all, it's good educational practice *and* good public relations to employ and document high-quality assessments. (And the PR pressure is ratcheted up when the state flouts the bedrock principles of the accountability agenda and what passes for educational common sense.) The problem, though, is that the QC were not developed for classroom assessments, but rather for large-scale assessments. As assessment expert Susan Brookhart (2003) recently has argued, the psychometric community has just begun to develop measurement theory appropriate to classroom assessment.[2]

Brookhart's challenge to the educational measurement community to work with educators to develop more appropriate metrics for classroom assessment is an important development because new, more sensitive tools to examine and document the quality of classroom assessment will allow its advocates to make a more broadly appealing case for it. For those teachers who routinely use what they know to be effective assessments in their classrooms, but who find that those assessments don't count in any real way outside the classroom, this development is a hopeful sign. It could, in fact, mark a turning point in how we think about who does assessment and what counts as good assessment.

As of this writing, the six QC are still the coin of the assessment quality realm in Nebraska. However, the state has undertaken two initiatives that mark a shift in its treatment of assessment quality. First, it is working with Brookhart to develop metrics amenable to classroom assessment. Second, as I described in Chapter 3, it is moving to cyclical on-site reviews instead of annual District Assessment Portfolios to allow context-sensitive examinations of each district's whole assessment process, including the decisions educators make based on assessment information. A heated debate rages within the state about the importance of traditional technical quality criteria, but in any case, Nebraska is pushing the psychometric community to engage teacher-designed classroom assessment.

In the meantime, what is happening with assessment in Nebraska schools? I devote the remainder of this section to identifying several trends across our study schools; the next section will take a more detailed look at how two teachers make assessment meaningful in their classrooms.

Developing Assessment Literacy

We saw in Chapter 3 that assessment quality ratings for District Assessment Portfolios rose sharply and steadily from 2000–2001 to 2004–5. While this trend, no doubt, is in part a function of districts' learning how to put together an effective portfolio, it is equally clear that Nebraska educators' assessment literacy has grown enormously.

While our early research revealed considerable, and predictable, unease about teachers' abilities to design, implement, interpret, and respond to high-quality assessment, over time teachers and administrators alike have become more knowledgeable about assessment and comfortable with their districts' assessment process. A typical teacher comment: "It's gotten easier and we've gotten better at looking at what needs to be changed and revised [in our curriculum and instruction]. . . . I've learned about . . . good question techniques, watching for biases, and just knowing what a good assessment looks like." Though districts are at different stages in the development of their assessment system, this principal articulates the general sentiment among educators in our study schools: "Definitely we're much more knowledgeable about what authentic assessment is and what is really reliable data."

Each year, our researchers noted increased sophistication among teachers about the purposes and uses of assessment, as well as the finer points of assessment design. Importantly, increasing numbers of teachers were coming to see assessment as meaningful to them in the classroom. "It's more beneficial to me," one teacher told us, "to assess the way I do now than I was last year, because I know how to use it or what to do with it." In particular, many teachers talked about how assessment has focused their attention on student *learning*, both in terms of groups within the classroom and in terms of individual students: "[STARS] has made us a lot more aware of what the standards are, how to measure them appropriately, and how to use the information from that measurement to plan what [each] child needs in instruction."

Some districts were designing their own assessments, and others were working with other districts as part of a consortium or (less formally) a collaboration. In the former instance, especially if the district was small, teachers were likely to be involved daily in the design, implementation, interpretation, and response to assessments. Teachers in consortium or collaboration schools were more likely to be involved only sporadically, and to draw from banks of items as they tailored their assessments to their classes. However, even teachers in large consortia sometimes felt intimately connected to the assessment process, as this teacher explains: "I'm very involved and I really feel a part of the whole assessment process. We get together as teachers from the districts in our area and make up tests and, you know, figure out the cut scores, and I just feel involved and really comfortable with the whole process that we go through." Of course, the creation of a criterion-referenced standards test at the consortium level harbors the same dangers a state test does. But only a handful of teachers in our study schools felt the consortium process did not honor their expertise or align to their local curriculum. Generally, these interdistrict partnerships were a means of sharing expertise and resources, rather than "contracting out" assessment and reporting (Isernhagen 2005). For example, one superintendent of a small school said, "We've learned that the consortium can help us with the technical aspects of [assessment] but that we need to really write assessments that fit with our curriculum."

Most assessment literacy in Nebraska is developed collaboratively, in teams of educators. While many districts have assessment coordinators, most districts' assessment process is the work of many hands. Through a variety of professional development offerings—workshops, data retreats, learning teams, summer academies, formal coursework—the state, districts, and regional support staff have built teacher expertise throughout the state. Using a "trainer of trainers" philosophy, Nebraska educators are spreading assessment literacy laterally, creating a "new breed of assessment literate educators" (Lukin et al. 2004, 31). Statewide efforts include

♦ the Nebraska Assessment Cohort Program, an eighteen-hour graduate endorsement at the University of Nebraska-Lincoln that trains educators to be assessment leaders in their districts;

♦ the Higher Education Assessment Framework, a set of guidelines regarding assessment literacy in preservice and graduate coursework for all seventeen Nebraska institutions of higher education with teacher education programs; and

♦ assessment literacy learning teams designed, in cooperation with Rick Stiggins' Assessment Training Institute, with the notion that teachers will engage in collaborative professional development around assessment.

Despite statewide and local efforts to increase assessment literacy among Nebraska educators, a great deal of work is yet to be done. In addition to the time factor discussed in Chapter 3, a significant challenge for STARS is the perception in many schools and districts that assessment is the purview of reporting-grade and reporting-subject teachers alone. For example, an elementary principal explained to us that his fourth-grade teachers continue to bear the brunt of assessment since assessment data are reported to the state at fourth grade. He's working to change the culture of the school so that "what happened in kindergarten, first, second, and third grade is part of the whole picture." But, he adds, "we're just not used to that." For this cultural shift to happen, teachers need to think of assessment as a shared responsibility, whether or not their data are reported to the state. In many of our study schools, we see this shift beginning, but it is evolutionary, rather than revolutionary.

Developing Instruction-Driven Assessment

For teachers experiencing assessment despair, the prospect of assessment literacy might sound more like a threat than an opportunity. Given the designs of the accountability agenda, they might reasonably worry that assessment literacy is really about holding teachers' collective feet to the technical fire, making them learn the lingo of psychometrics in order to norm them to the expectations of yet another group of outsiders who have designs on their classrooms. But while it's true that Nebraska teachers are being asked to engage the psychometric concepts enshrined in the six QC, the pressure is also moving in the opposite direction; that is, teachers and their classroom assessments are causing the psychometric community to rethink its assumptions and practices. Moreover, the assessments in use in Nebraska schools are not designed by psychometricians, but by teachers. They are driven by instruction, embedded in curriculum, and reliant on teachers' professional judgment.

Our researchers' first indication that this was so was something of a surprise. In an early round of surveys, teachers reported few *major* changes in curriculum or instruction after the implementation of their district's assessment program. No matter what topic we asked teachers about—numeration, measurement, geometry, and spatial concepts in math, for instance—the majority reported placing the *same emphasis* on them after the implementation of their local assessments as they had before.

It wasn't until our follow-up interviews that we realized why this was the case. This teacher explains:

> We didn't change our curriculum and standards because our curriculum we consider[ed] sound to begin with. We found projects, ideas, things that we did within our curriculum already and found places where they met the standards... We didn't find it necessary to contort or twist or... force what we teach to the standards or force the standards to what we teach.

The process this teacher describes—designing *out* from the classroom rather than *down* from standards or assessments—was common in our study schools.

In practical terms, the embedding of assessments in curriculum and instruction generally means that schools are refusing (or moving away from) traditional lengthy end-of-unit (or quarter- or year-end) tests and moving toward more frequent, ongoing assessments. In the past, as one superintendent explained, educators would wait for results of a standardized test, "hope it didn't look too bad, and put it away." By contrast, ongoing, local assessment is "causing us...to rethink and relook at the way we organize instruction." A teacher in another district told us, "What we really wanted to get away from was the high-stakes assessment when kids are just tested once a year, and everything is determined on that one particular test. We wanted it to be ongoing, about what is going on in the classroom on a daily basis, to assess what they know and what they've mastered through what we've taught them." Many Nebraska educators talk about "the instructional loop": design, implementation, assessment.

Some schools were breaking up assessments and administering them throughout the year: "[We] have moved from taking two weeks out of the year and giving kids tests to looking at our curriculum and matching the components of the test to meet the curriculum." Granted, there is a danger here that schools will simply *give more tests*. In a handful of our study schools—such as the one in which a language arts teacher administered eight separate tests on the same standard—this was the case. But in most schools, we saw teachers using multiple kinds of assessments, including informal teacher observations and writing activities, in a strategic way throughout the school year. In fact, several of our study schools *reduced* the number of formal tests they gave when their teachers expanded their assessment repertoires and when they moved away—as several schools did—from reliance on tests and textbooks as guideposts for curriculum and instruction. These schools were often able to ratchet down the testing pressure on students, as assessment became "just another activity to do and another practice for [students]." Several teachers talked about the importance of "demystifying" assessment to the extent that students didn't even know when they were being formally assessed and when they were simply carrying out "regular" classroom activities.

Almost all the teachers in our study believed that locally designed assessments were far more useful for instruction than national, norm-referenced tests. When asked to compare the two types of assessments, both math and reading teachers rated their local assessments considerably higher than norm-referenced tests for evaluating student progress, assessing teaching effectiveness, and planning instruction (Bandalos 2003). In addition, teachers valued the *ongoing* nature of their districts' assessment program: "If you're looking at a one-time-only test, the kids don't learn much from that assessment. When you're doing the ongoing assessments, where the kids look at the feedback, they turn around before the next time and they think, 'OK, what can we work on to improve for next time?'" Many teachers spoke about the importance—for students and teachers—of immediate feedback: "It's a real value that we're providing instant feedback to our students about how well they performed, and we're using that information to directly perfect our instruction. It's not a matter of an outside group assessing our students and then telling us how they did."

Using Assessment to Focus Teaching and Learning

While instruction drives assessment in many Nebraska schools, assessment in turn informs instruction. Teachers systematically gather data on individual students and groups of students and make instructional decisions based on those data. They know where their students are succeeding and where they are struggling. They know performance trends in their school over time. They know about achievement gaps. And they are coming to know which of their interventions are working and which are not.

In our third round of interviews, in 2004, our researchers set out to examine what Nebraska educators were doing with the data they had collected. While some schools, predictably, struggled with data overload after collecting much more information than they needed, most were at least beginning to use data to develop and refine their curriculum, instruction, professional development programs, and assessment programs (Gallagher 2004a). In each area, the emphasis was on increasing *focus* so that the various activities of the school were coordinated and (re)directed toward their shared emphasis: teaching and learning. Curricular gaps were being eliminated, instructional redundancies were being reduced, professional development was becoming more relevant to the issues faced by the school, and assessment was becoming more ongoing.

The 2004 interviews, when compared with previous rounds, revealed heightened attention to particular groups of students, including low-income students, English language learners, and ethnic or racial groups. At the same time, teachers talked a great deal about individualizing instruction. In both cases, we saw movement away from prepackaged curricula, textbooks, and large tests and toward flexible, adaptive, teacher-designed instructional and curricular programs. Perhaps for this reason, we also observed increased attention to instructional research. This teacher's comment is typical:

> We wouldn't be teachers if we didn't know how to teach. But actually breaking things apart and really using effective strategies, I think, is the key. . . . And that might not have been a real strength for some teachers. [But] now . . . we're making it part of our whole school, that process where teachers are learning the best practices and implementing them into their classrooms.

While all of our study schools found plenty of room for improvement, their instruction-driven process allowed them to identify and enhance their strengths as well.

Our study included a small number of exceptions: schools that sacrificed what they knew to be strong projects in favor of what were perceived to be more easily measurable curricula and instruction. A principal in a school with a strong tradition of community-based education, for instance, stated that "it takes too much time to develop assessments to match those [community-based] projects . . . We've lost some of that neat stuff that we were doing and getting kids into the community and community members into the school." Meanwhile, teachers in large schools and districts sometimes felt alienated from core decisions about curriculum and instruction. Here, district objectives, large criterion-referenced tests, and textbooks continued to dictate the curriculum. Coverage—at a pace set by the central office—was prized over deep learning. Teachers in these schools reported moving through the curriculum more quickly than they would if their professional judgment were their guide. One teacher suggested that "we could extend the learning by doing more exploratory learning or more constructivist learning but . . . that takes time. So we find . . . the best way to get this amount covered."

Once again, STARS provides an opportunity for Nebraska schools to escape the most regressive features of the accountability agenda, but it does not guarantee that result. Assessment will drive instruction if educators let it. Although the state must continue to make STARS as manageable as possible, the fate of Nebraska's school-based, teacher-led experiment hinges largely on decisions made at the local level.

Moving (Slowly) Toward Student-Involved Assessment

The significance of local decision making could not be clearer than in the disparate experiences of Nebraska students. For some students, by their teachers' reckoning, life is not markedly different than it would be in a state with state tests: "You know, they spend all this time and worry and try to do well [on tests], and then they don't ever find out how they did"; "Students are numb with all these CRTs [criterion-referenced tests]." Students (like teachers) don't care if the Big Test comes from the district office, the state capital, or Washington, D.C., if it is not connected to what they do in the classroom—if it doesn't emerge organically from that work.

Commissioner Christensen and the Nebraska Department of Education understand the potential for assessment to cause student (and teacher) disengagement. In response to President Bush's proposed expansion of NCLB to include regular testing in high schools, Christensen stated that simply adding standardized tests "flies in the face of all the research that shows that the problem with our high schools is disconnected kids. I don't know how testing is going to connect them; it seems to me it would disconnect them" (in Nordby 2005, 1A). Instead, Christensen would rather see locally developed assessments used as part of a concerted effort to connect students and schools to their communities. This is why Nebraska has put so much energy and so many resources into classroom assessment, from working with the educational measurement community on new metrics, to the assessment literacy initiatives described earlier, to the development of practical print and online resources, to a partnership with Rick Stiggins (2004b), a pioneer of "student-involved assessment."

Stiggins' (2005) vision of "student-involved assessment FOR learning" enlists students as partners with their teachers in setting learning goals, monitoring their own progress, making decisions based on information they gather about their learning, and communicating evidence of their learning to others. According to Stiggins, when students are engaged in this way in their own learning, their motivation and their achievement levels rise dramatically. Like traditional conceptions of formative assessment, student-involved assessment provides teachers with information about student learning; however, Stiggins' approach also shines a light on what *students* do with that information.

Our researchers observed the influence of Stiggins' approach in several schools that used student portfolios similar to those in Mr. Sands' school (Chapter 2). Teachers in these schools talked about developing an "individual education plan for each student," noting the portfolios allowed students to track their own progress and make decisions about their learning. These portfolios were sometimes organized by standard so students would know where they were vis-à-vis that set of expectations. Teachers talked about these portfolios as maps to help students "gauge where they're at, where they're going, [and] what they need to do to get there."

In addition to student portfolios, teachers talked about using rubrics (scoring guides) in classrooms and in particular creating student-friendly rubrics to help students understand learning expectations. They emphasized the importance of developing a "shared language" about learning: "The more teachers talk to the kids, the more the kids want to know how they have done and what they need to improve on. So that has opened up a lot of communication between the two."

This practice was particularly prevalent in the area of writing. Again, Nebraska uses the familiar Six Traits writing rubric for its annual statewide writing assessment at grades 4, 8, and 11. Teachers consistently reported in interviews that they asked students to use the language of the Six Traits—ideas, voice, organization, word choice, sentence fluency, conventions—to assess their own and each other's writing. One teacher told us, "[W]hen you teach that way, they [students] learn to know what good writing looks like." Another added that asking students to apply assessment language to real writing— their own and their peers'—helps them "to take responsibility for their own learning."

In short, many teachers testified that students become more motivated, critical, and reflective learners when they are invited into the assessment experience. They talked with special enthusiasm about using performance assessments to move students beyond rote memorization toward application and self-evaluation. In several schools, assessments now typically involve a reflective component in which students articulate the *significance* of what they know and can do as well as set their own learning goals. These schools are leading a steady, if slow, movement among Nebraska schools in the direction of student-involved assessment.

Overcoming Assessment Despair: Portraits of Assessment as Classroom Practice

In his contribution to a book called *Letters to the Next President*, Nebraska teacher Edward Montgomery wrote:

> Three years ago, I despised the idea of assessment. Today, I run the system for my district and work in a new administrative position we didn't even have back then, in addition to my regular teaching duties. The key element that converted me was *teacher involvement*. (2004, 160)

Ed's "conversion," while more dramatic than most, is representative of teachers in our study in this sense: Those teachers who were actively involved in their district's assessment process generally reported more confidence in their teaching and a higher sense of efficacy than did teachers who did not participate in those processes. In other words, teacher involvement in assessment often led to increased teacher engagement.

Ed is by his own reckoning a "typical" Nebraska teacher. He teaches high school English in a small town located in a sparsely populated county, both called Kimball. Three times its present size during the oil and missile boom of the 1960s, Kimball is now in economic dire straits. The families, almost all white, generally service wells for a depressed oil industry or struggle to keep wheat crops viable. (Kimball's claim to fame is the highest point in the state; residents like to say, "From here, it's downhill to Denver." But the joke is probably less than amusing to the families struggling to keep crops alive a mile above sea level in this water-thirsty area.)

The Kimball school system consists of three buildings and serves 650 students, K–12. Thirty-four percent of those students qualify for free or reduced lunch. Although Kimball students generally achieve well, Ed reports that about a third of his class was "not proficient" on the eleventh-grade Statewide Writing Assessment in 2004.

In the piece that follows, Ed shares a strategy for making creative (perhaps subversive) use of the Six Traits writing rubric. Readers might find it strange that I highlight in this example the features of STARS that look the most like what is happening in other states: the SWA and Six Traits. But doing so allows me to underscore an important point: There is more than one way for teachers to reclaim assessment as classroom practice. Ed shows how teachers can use existing assessment instruments to develop responsible, responsive, student-involved classroom assessment. Then Suzanne Ratzlaff will share an assessment that she developed with her colleague and fourth-grade students. Both teachers—neither of whom works in one of our study schools—show what happens when teachers conquer assessment despair and make assessment meaningful in the classroom.

Edward Montgomery, High School Teacher, Kimball Public Schools

My classroom is process based, as I think every writing class should be. I serve a variety of students, many of them at risk. It is therefore vital that our students understand the traits found in the model Nebraska uses: ideas, organization, voice, word choice, fluency, and conventions. *However, rather than have students write to meet the needs of a rubric, I teach students to use the rubric to meet their needs as writers and readers.* We do this by scoring pieces of literature according to the same rubric the students are scored by. They discover and describe the strengths, and sometimes the weaknesses, of using a rubric for producing and evaluating writing. In this way, we address Nebraska's writing and reading standards.

I call this activity Rate the Writers. Early in the year, the Six Traits are reintroduced. We then read "Logging and Pimping," by Norman Maclean (the title alone gets them interested). The students are then asked to write a short essay analyzing the story according to the same rubric used to grade their material. They score it on a grade sheet with comments and use the grade sheet as notes for their essays.

After the essays are completed, we have a roundtable discussion to compare the scores they gave in each trait and then the overall score they gave the story. The discussion takes off as they find themselves arguing and defending positions based on the language of the rubric. Most often students have very solid, defensible criticisms of the story and they come up with the same criticisms that Maclean's editor voiced. Maclean himself said the story is not very good and I show the students the comments the author made later about his early work. The students are surprised and pleased that they and the author identified the same strengths and weaknesses in the piece.[3]

The next reading assignment is Maclean's masterpiece, *A River Runs Through It*. I have never had students who did not love this novel. They are asked to compare it with the earlier story, score it with the rubric, and then write an analytical essay. Not only do we discuss the rubric, but we also discuss how the rubric makes it hard to score items, such as the passion that comes through in *A River Runs Through It*. Is this ideas, voice, word choice, or a combination? Again the discussions are rewarding. Students come in the next year asking to read the stories because they have heard the positive reviews from previous students.

As the students do other assignments, they can talk knowledgeably about their writing and the writing of their classmates. They analyze strengths and weaknesses when we review their work together. They have a better knowledge of writing and literary analysis as a result of this activity. The key to this activity is giving students the freedom to score the authors. It makes the authors into real, approachable writers who struggled and made choices in their writing just as the students have to in their writing.

It should be emphasized that this activity is a tool for the class; teaching to the rubric is not the goal! As the year goes by, students question the limitations of the rubric, especially in the area of ideas. The rubric serves as a starting place, not a finishing line. In fact, the rubric goes unmentioned late in the year because we are concentrating more on areas that a rubric has difficulty capturing. Student writing has met and surpassed the rubric. This is the development I am striving for; I want them to go beyond the rubric.

As a result of this activity, students become self-assessors and they have more confidence in their knowledge of the traits found in good writing. My students become good critics; many progress to the point where they can tell me why a piece of writing is good even though they may not like it personally. This knowledge carries over into their other classes. Students find they can debate the merits of any piece of writing and that their positions need to be well informed. They can also tell me when and why the rubric helps them and when it limits them. We discuss the good and bad points of a rubric and exactly what the rubric does and does not say.

This simple little tool has made my composition class popular and freed me from being the sole judge of student writing. By the time a student and I work through a piece of writing, we generally agree on what is in it and how we feel about the quality. I find that we eventually spend our discussion time on the more abstract concepts involved in good writing because the basics have taken of themselves.

Suzanne Ratzlaff is a fourth-grade teacher in Heartland Community Schools in east-central Nebraska. Like Ed—and many Nebraska teachers—she lives and works in a small town, in this case Henderson, population 986. In 1998, the schools in Henderson and Bradshaw (population 336) consolidated to create Heartland Community, which serves 331 students, K–12. The Henderson-Bradshaw area is largely working-class, though it has a strong educational, health, and social services sector, including a regional hospital located in Henderson.

Heartland Community Schools is well known around the state for its stellar teaching staff and its students' high achievement. Many Heartland teachers, including Suzanne, have been active in professional networks such as the School at the Center rural education program and the National Writing Project. Heartland teachers are leaders in community-based education. In fact, largely on the strength of her community-based projects, Suzanne was named Nebraska Teacher of the Year in 2003.

Suzanne Ratzlaff, Fourth-Grade Teacher, Heartland Community Schools

As a teacher, have you ever experienced that extraordinary moment when the students in your classroom are so actively involved in the learning process, so independently engaged in the academic experience, that you merely become a bystander and are no longer needed? It is awesome. That was something I was not willing to give up when creating our district's local assessments matching the Nebraska state standards. I could not lose those authentic, purposeful learning experiences and replace them with sterile fill-in-the-blank, matching, and multiple-choice assessments.

Fourth-grade teachers are required to assess many standards yearly. However, I am privileged to teach in a state that believes in the power of the classroom teacher, recognizing it is the teacher who holds the key to making a positive impact on learning. I was also blessed to be part of Nebraska's Goals 2000 Assessment Project, where classroom teachers gathered to look at their authentic learning projects, find the many state standards embedded throughout them, and create assessments matching these learning experiences to the Nebraska state standards.

My assessment designing began with fellow teacher Rod Diercks during an Action Research project and continued with fourth-grade teacher Deb Friesen, as we worked with a passion designing student-friendly research assessment guides [see Figure 4–2]. These guides were created for students to use while researching topics related to a variety of subject areas, as well as place-based education. Along with written indicators, there are multiple drawings, which represent information and expectations of the research process. All quality indicators are written in student words, and each state standard being assessed is printed at the bottom of the guide and worded in student-friendly language. Our goal is that all children understand everything on the rubric.

Student-friendly assessment guides are invaluable. Not only are students being assessed on specific state standards; they are learning the skills of self-assessment. Children today are growing up in a visual world, and the drawings help them see and understand what is expected.

These classroom assessments are under continuous revision with input from the students as well as from teacher observation and evaluation of students' progress. For example, the earliest rubrics were designed with the lowest score point on the left and the highest on the right. Students asked, "Why do you have us read the worst first? Since we read from the left to the right, why don't you have the highest score on the left so we can read what is the best right away?" That became our first big change. The students also helped clarify the quality indicators and standard descriptions to be more student friendly.

The drawings also needed modifications. We discovered what you draw is what you get. Rod and I had observed a few students sitting at their computers, eyes closed and thinking. After we asked what they were doing, they replied they were writing their research reports. When we looked at our written report assessment guide, we understood what had happened. The drawing was of a student sitting at a computer, eyes closed, with a thought balloon filled with a list of the steps of research. As a result, we modified the drawing by adding a research binder and data notes next to the computer and we made

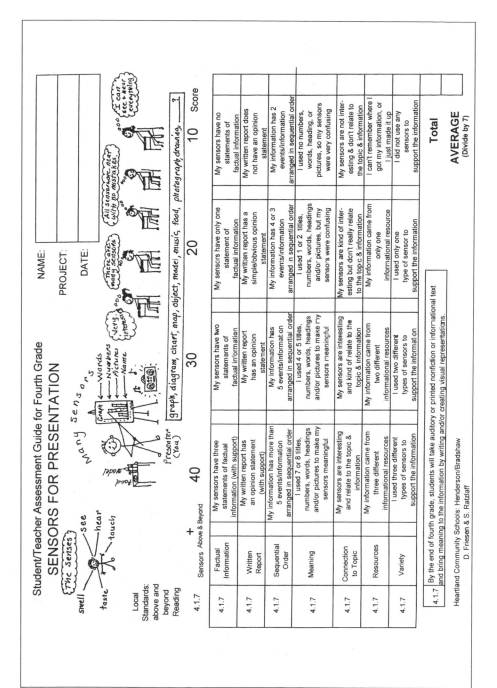

Figure 4–2 *Student-Friendly Rubric*

sure our stick figure had open eyes. I guess you could say that as teachers, our eyes were also opened that day.

We made one further modification when a fellow Action Researcher asked us, "What happens if a student goes beyond the expectations of the rubric?" We went back to our classrooms and put this question to our students. The group came up with the idea of having a section to the left of the highest quality indicator, and this became our "Above and Beyond" column. We chose to leave this section blank because there are unlimited possibilities of what could be achieved when going above and beyond. It would be the students who would create and design their own performances and products.

When students are given multiple opportunities to work through and bring meaning to these research guides, the quality of their final research projects is exceptional. Therefore, the quality indicators on each rubric have extremely high expectations for fourth-grade elementary students. Yet, with guidance, all students become active learners and reach these high standards. They take ownership of their learning and become self-assessors.

There will always be a few students who need to be reminded to find their rubrics or may lose them completely. These students need to work individually with a teacher to develop their own words and pictures, creating personal assessment guides. When a student needs to bring more meaning to the rubrics, we talk through the visual representations (drawings), have him or her reinterpret the information, and we add more visuals. We do the same with the quality indicators.

There are times when I wonder if it might have been easier to just administer traditional, isolated skill assessments, or maybe simply one statewide test and be done with it. Truthfully, that would have been the easy way out, yet it would not have made such a strong, positive impact on the learning of my students. Nebraska risked complexity with STARS and engaged every classroom teacher across the state. We became the evaluators, assessors, and specialists. However, Rod, Deb, and I carried it a bit further and risked even more complexity by engaging every student in our classrooms, helping them become their own evaluators, assessors, and specialists. They now hold the key to unlock their own minds and make a positive impact on their learning. That is the power of self-assessment.

It would be misleading (despite Ed's claim to the contrary) to suggest that Ed and Suzanne are typical Nebraska teachers. In fact, I've chosen them because they are extraordinarily articulate about what they do. But what's most exciting about these teachers' work is not that it represents some sort of transportable best practice—a dangerously static concept—but rather that it illustrates what becomes possible when teachers and students are engaged together in meaningful classroom assessment.

Twenty-First-Century Assessment

Nebraska teachers have come a long way in what is, in school reform terms, a blink of an eye. In five years, their assessment literacy has grown to unprecedented levels. And it continues to grow and adapt as more teachers learn how to involve students in assessment. In fact, Nebraska teachers are leading the way toward a new generation of assessment theory and practice. The state has created the conditions for teacher-designed assessment to flourish—and to count. But a new generation of assessment will require new assessment tools, and those tools must come from teachers.

As we see in Ed's and Suzanne's examples, most teachers begin with familiar tools: rubrics. Both teachers show that rubrics can be useful tools for generating a shared language in the classroom and for involving students in self-assessment. But as teachers well know, rubrics can go horribly wrong. Suzanne recently wrote to me,

> You can lock students into matching the rubric. Once, I created a rubric specifically for a presentation board, drawing the display board with detailed examples of pictures, documents, captions, headings, etc. And guess what? Almost every student matched the rubric. The boards were well done, but they all looked the same. Boring! So, the next year, I used the rubric again but emphasized that this was just one example, and they could be inventive when creating their boards. And it happened again. Most of the boards still looked the same. So, I quit using that rubric. (personal correspondence, 3/15/06)

As Suzanne recognizes, involving students in assessment is salutary if it allows them to examine critically and question others' expectations and to devise their own learning goals. But it is repressive if it merely makes them more dutiful hoop jumpers. Rubrics potentially endanger meaningful engagement with student work in favor of clean categories that allow for consistency in scoring (Wilson 2006; Broad 2003). What students most need is rich response to their work, not a number that quantifies what is finally unquantifiable. As Maja Wilson argues, a reductive assessment tool is a reductive assessment tool, no matter who designs it (2006, 57).[4] Teacher-designed, student-involved assessment has enormous potential, but it does not *guarantee* engagement. Teachers are just as capable as psychometricians or corporate test makers of designing poor assessments that atomize learning and make it static and meaningless to students. In fact, student-involved assessment could become nothing more (or less) than a requirement to parrot standards or rubric language that students don't care about or even understand. In this case, student-involved assessment becomes a particularly pernicious form of surveillance and behavior management—much like teacher-involved standards and assessment that do not move beyond tokenism and cherry picking. Both activities amount to enlisting people in their own oppression.

However, the "radical," hopeful message of STARS is that teachers, not outside "experts," *are* the right people to give shape to the next generation of educational assessment. After all, they are the ones who spend their days with students, who understand the human dimensions of teaching and learning, who know—in short—how to practice the arts of classroom engagement.

Notes

1. As hopeful as this development sounds, Patricia Lynne (2004) argues compellingly that we—teachers, particularly writing specialists—ought to be skeptical about the potential for traditional psychometrics to serve our needs. Indeed, Lynne argues that we need a new assessment vocabulary that will allow us to sever ties with an outmoded and harmfully reductive "objectivist paradigm" (42). While I view this thesis as provocative, I find her conclusion—that writing specialists ought to step away from the assessment conversation, come up with a set of our own terms, and only then return to the table—for all its considerable attractions, to be both logistically untenable (how can a whole discipline move as one?) and politically dangerous (what happens to kids and teachers in the meantime?).

2. Although Brookhart does not discuss this, the psychometric concept that needs the most attention is *reliability*. As Broad (2003), Wilson (2006), Huot (2002), and others have argued, insistence on reader agreement (interrater reliability) often leads us to require only simple (often vapid) work from students.

3. In the acknowledgment section of *A River Runs Through It*, Maclean admits that in "Logging and Pimping," "[he] was concentrating so on telling a story that [he] didn't take time to be a poet and express a little of the love [he has] of the earth" (1992, xiv). This is the same conclusion that my students come to; the first story has all the elements of a good story, but something is missing, which you can find in *River*.

4. As a writing teacher myself, I bristle at the reduction of this deeply human, complex, and context-bound practice to a short list of textual features that students may well come to believe encompass everything they need to know about writing. See Gallagher 2002a, Chapter 3, for my full critique of Nebraska's approach to writing assessment.

Engaging Colleagues
Creating New Models of
Professional Development

Regional Inservice, Anywhere, USA

The auditorium—buzzing with chatter and the occasional whoop of laughter—has the look and feel of a school assembly. Only this time, the bleachers are filled with teachers from this and neighboring schools. For the most part, they seem to be enjoying each other's company as they balance cups of coffee on notebooks and gnaw at their donuts. But there's a palpable impatience in the room—unsurprisingly, as today (a minor holiday) was supposed to be a day off.

As the featured presenter begins, the clamor slowly dies down. And all at once—almost as if an invisible puppeteer has slackened his strings—hundreds of teachers lean their backs against the benches behind them and slump their shoulders. Eyes quickly glazing over, they assume the classic pose of bored teenagers. Even the few who jot notes (or are they doodling?) on the Seven Keys or the Five Strategies or the Nine Best Practices look disconnected, shut down. None of the speaker's bold promises—Tailored to *any* school context! Aligned to state standards! Better living through online technology! You're in control!—rouses the teachers from their semislumber.

Finally finished, the speaker is offered tepid applause. The administrator: "Wow. This gives us a lot to think about. *(Pause.)* I see by my watch that it is almost three o'clock. The bell should ring in a minute. I hope today has been helpful to you. Remember, you are the key to unlocking students' success."

With that, the reanimated teachers leap from their crouched positions to join a ritual this auditorium has seen many times before: the Friday afternoon stampede.

———◆◆◆———

Engaging Professional Development

While the details of this scenario are fictional, I've attended several sessions like it, and I'd wager it's familiar, in its general outlines, to most teachers. Schools and districts organize inservices around talking heads and most service providers dispense one-size-fits-all "best practices." Administrators make an appearance at these events—and then quickly retreat to their offices to get on with "their" work. Teachers collect their professional development chits until they reach their annual quotas. And everyone goes through the motions, as if these one-time, get-it-and-go events really made much of a difference in the lives of teachers and their students.

The accountability agenda and No Child Left Behind have only made matters worse. The accountability agenda encourages states to focus their resources on building remote-control systems run by external "experts": administrators, policymakers, politicians, curriculum designers, textbook companies, testing firms. Instead of promoting rich professional development to build teacher expertise, it attempts an end run around teachers. To the extent that this agenda pays any attention to professional development, it focuses educators' efforts on increasing test scores by training them in test prep and narrow, allegedly transportable strategies for improving achievement. More and more professional development—like more and more education generally—is being prepackaged for teachers by profiteering service providers whose slick, teacher-proof pitches make it frighteningly easy to imagine a day when professional development isn't needed at all, as teaching will be reduced to script reading and test administration.

Of course, NCLB has generated some high-minded rhetoric around "highly qualified teachers." But it defines that term narrowly around subject-area knowledge (Berry, Hoke, and Hirsch 2004).[1] There are a number of problems with this conflation of expertise with content knowledge, however commonsensical the idea might sound. First, it suggests subject knowledge is sufficient, when any teacher worth her salt knows this knowledge must be combined with pedagogical theory and practice: a deep understanding of schooling, learning, child development, and practical experience. Second, narrowing professional development to content knowledge de-emphasizes ongoing teacher learning. It imagines teachers as repositories of information, not as lifelong learners who model learning for students. Third, this conflation defines professional development as an *individual* endeavor—a matter of racking up the requisite credentials to be deemed highly qualified. Once again, the accountability agenda, for all its bluster about rigorous standards, asks far too *little* of teachers and schools.

Is it any wonder, then, that many teachers regard professional development as a cynical game at best and a bitter joke at worst? Is it any wonder they sit through their professional development hours and then return to their classrooms, close their doors, and ignore what they've been told by an expert who's often never stepped foot in their classroom and never will? After all, teachers are experts in *learning*; they know that these "learning opportunities" fly in the face of the core principle that people learn best when they construct their own knowledge through meaningful activities connected to things they care about (Resnick and Hall 1998; Robb 2000). They know, too, that despite all the admonitions about working with colleagues to make the ideas shared in inservices their own, the seeds-to-the-wind model doesn't work: once the inservice is over, life in the school quickly returns more or less to normal.

But you don't have to be a learning expert to see that this model of professional development doesn't work.[2] *Everyone* knows it doesn't work. Writing in 1999, for instance, Willis Hawley and Linda Vallie outlined an "almost unprecedented consensus" among researchers, professional development specialists, and policymakers about the characteristics of effective professional development: it (1) is driven by analyses of the relationship between student learning goals and actual student performance; (2) asks teachers to identify their learning needs and to participate, when possible, in the development of the activities; (3) is site based; (4) is organized around collaborative problem solving; (5) is "continuous and ongoing"; (6) involves analyses of multiple sources of information; (7) helps teachers develop a theoretical understanding of what is to be learned; and (8) is "integrated with a comprehensive change process" (138). That few of these principles are regularly practiced nearly a decade later borders on tragic.

So why *shouldn't* teachers protect themselves and their students from these ridiculous demands and these poor excuses for learning opportunities? Why *not* close their doors and get on with the real business of teaching and learning?

While these responses are reasonable in light of the relentless assault of the accountability agenda on teachers' professionalism, and while subterfuge is sometimes necessary in an oppressive system, we also know that meaningful school improvement—the kind that supports student learning—hinges on *teacher* learning (McLaughlin and Oberman 1996, x; see also Darling-Hammond and Sykes 1999 and Robb 2000). Teachers who are lifelong learners are best able to help their students become the same. In order for that to happen, they must throw open those classroom doors.

But what's on the other side of those doors? Too often, as we've seen, it's a chorus of experts telling teachers what to do. What teachers *should* find are collegial, personally meaningful conversations and activities that actually benefit kids. These authentic conversations and activities should make teachers feel more like professionals, more connected to the core work of their schools—and less alone.

This is the promise of Nebraska's STARS. It explains why the Nebraska State Board of Education has set the goal of 100 percent teacher participation in the process. It explains why the state and most of its districts treat professional development not as a mark of individual accomplishment, but rather a tool for teacher engagement: a means by which teachers learn continuously from each other and build capacity together. And it explains the considerable resources Nebraska has devoted to helping teachers do just that.

In previous chapters, I've mentioned several initiatives the Nebraska Department of Education has undertaken to support and spread assessment literacy among teachers throughout the state: new preservice requirements in assessment; an assessment leadership endorsement program for teachers and administrators; numerous interactive trainings, workshops, and "data retreats" in concert with assessment expert Rick Stiggins and regional educational service units (ESUs); consultative school visits; electronic and paper resources for classroom-based assessment; STARS grants to support local work on standards and assessment; and (soon) onsite reviews to provide not only summative ratings on assessment quality but also formative feedback on assessment, instruction, curriculum, and school improvement. In fact, I could cite many more. But what's important here is that these are more than a ragtag collection of activities; rather, they constitute a statewide professional development program that enacts two core principles: *teachers teaching teachers* and *embedded professional development*.

The first principle is about cultivating local talent deliberately and exponentially. Virtually everything the Nebraska Department of Education and its partners (ESUs and districts) do in this area employs a trainer-of-trainers model that makes use of existing expertise while constantly cycling new people into the process. Unlike the seeds-to-the-wind notion that informs traditional professional development, the idea here is that once trained, teachers and administrators have a responsibility to help train others, and structures are set up to ensure that this happens in a systematic way. Not only is this an efficient way to reach remote or large numbers of teachers, but it also increases the chances that teachers will buy in to the process, as they are participants in and developers of it.

As crucial as this principle is for building and spreading expertise among teachers, it is not enough. After all, expertise is only as meaningful as what teachers *do* with it in specific sites of practice. Hence the second principle, which insists that teacher expertise be further shaped, extended, and perhaps revised within school contexts. This is why the trainer-of-trainers model is combined with a learning teams approach. NDE has supported learning teams as a professional development tool since the inception of STARS.[3] Its early work with Stiggins used the trainer-of-trainers model to build local learning teams. It has also provided STARS grants for the development of district and school learning teams.

It is important to understand these two principles—*teachers teaching teachers* and *embedded professional development*—as complementary. Unless teacher expertise is embedded in and shaped by the ongoing work of the school, it is unlikely to make a meaningful difference for teachers and kids. But unless that ongoing work is informed by regular infusions of fresh teacher expertise, it runs the risk of becoming insular, even parochial. The combination of these two principles makes Nebraska's professional development program dynamic and locally meaningful, and it places Nebraska in the vanguard of next-generation professional development. It imagines professional development as a tool for engagement—the building of meaningful relationships—among educators. And as Figure 5–1 demonstrates, this approach is distinct from, and in many ways reverses, that of the accountability agenda.

Professional Development in Nebraska Schools

Although Nebraska schools only recently became involved in the professional learning communities (PLCs) movement, our researchers have observed the key characteristics of learning communities in the state's schools for some time. Shirley Hord, an influential researcher of PLCs, identifies those characteristics as (1) supportive and shared leadership; (2) shared values and vision; (3) collective learning and application of that learning; (4) supportive conditions; and (5) shared

Two Views of Professional Development	
Accountability	**Engagement**
Individual	Collaborative
Content based	Comprehensive
Event oriented	Ongoing
Compliance focus	Commitment focus
Data driven	Data informed
One size fits all	Context sensitive
"Best practices" focus	Embedded in schools
Sit 'n' git	Interactive, participatory
Outside experts	Teachers teaching teachers

Figure 5–1 Two Views of Professional Development

personal practice (2004, 1). A few Nebraska schools evinced all these characteristics quite strongly; most were stronger on some characteristics than others. Overall, the first three were most in evidence in our study schools, while the fourth and especially the fifth were only sometimes apparent. But the point is that almost all our study schools were moving in the direction mapped out by the literature on PLCs (in addition to Hord, see Cochran-Smith and Lytle 1993; Darling-Hammond and Sykes 1999; *Educational Leadership* May 2004; Goldenberg 2004; Huffman and Hipp 2003; Hargreaves 1995; McLaughlin and Oberman 1996; McLaughlin and Talbert 2001; Robb 2000; Sergiovanni 1994; and Weinbaum et al. 2004). Moreover, they were doing so as part of a statewide effort to connect professional development to standards and assessment, a focus largely absent from the PLC literature.[4]

The cultural shift toward collaborative professional development was so pronounced in our study schools that we often heard the phrase *teacher in private practice* used as an epithet to describe a colleague who refused to participate in collaborative school improvement activities. Again and again, we talked with teachers who had come to believe that when all educators in a school pull in the same direction, they are better able to meet the needs of kids and improve their school. Those teachers who were most active in this process also had the highest sense of self-efficacy because, they said, they understood the crucial role they played in students' success.

Within the general cultural shift I'm describing, we identified several trends across our study schools.

Generating Regular, Focused Professional Conversations

Among Nebraska teachers, the most consistently cited benefit of STARS was the development of what one teacher called "intense professional conversations"—often for the first time in anyone's institutional memory. This description is typical: "everybody is more focused and working on the same [page] rather than everybody just working on their own little space and [saying], 'Don't bother me.'" Sometimes, the conversations were formally structured by learning teams, regular grade-level and content-area meetings, curriculum mapping sessions, assessment design or data interpretation meetings, and so on. But we heard as well about less formal but ubiquitous professional conversations during, before, and after the school day.

Two features of these conversations are worth special note. First, they were focused on *student learning*, the new lingua franca for Nebraska teachers. As a result, they were more focused on patterns in student achievement, instructional strategies (including remediation and enrichment), curriculum design, and of course assessment. A fourth-grade teacher, for instance, reported that grade-level meetings "have been very helpful because we discuss strategies on what can we do or what [we] are...doing in [our] classrooms." Although many teachers, by their own admission, only reluctantly opened their classroom doors, they did so when they saw that their students benefited. By way of example, several teachers cited the discovery, once they started talking to other teachers, that they were all teaching pet projects—dinosaurs, for instance, or the weather cycle—but that students needed a more coherent, sequenced curriculum to grow as learners.

This last point leads to the second important feature of these collegial conversations: They enhanced teachers' sense of *professionalism*. After all, as we heard from teachers around the state, a mark of teacher professionalism is an unrelenting focus on student learning. This commitment led many teachers to seek out more professional resources; for instance, one teacher and assessment coordinator told us, "we pay more attention to articles, we pay more attention to conferences on assessment, [and] we seek out additional information hoping to help our school..., our teachers, and ultimately...our students." At the same time, many teachers were also coming to value what *they* brought to the table: "I feel as if my voice, it matters, that what I feel is best for students is being brought up in meetings and I'm able to discuss my opinions with other teachers and we can bounce ideas off one another." Some Nebraska teachers call these "million-dollar conversations."

I don't think this economic metaphor is an accident. The phrase signals a high *return* on what is, admittedly, an investment: these conversations require both time and money. And it won't be immediately apparent to every administrator or policymaker why he or she should invest in what sounds like a mundane and seemingly low-yield activity: sitting and talking. But that's just it: The benefits of the intense professional conversations, according to these teachers, are far more significant than the traditional professional development activities that have drained district coffers for years. As one assessment coordinator put it, "our days of sending people off to workshops at the most desirable locations to just attend a buffet [are over]"; professional development is now focused around the specific needs of individual schools and districts.

Fostering Teacher Commitment

Once again taking a page from the accountability agenda's book (ledger?), I extend the economic metaphor: When teachers experience "million-dollar conversations," they are likely to take ownership in the process. A teacher explained: "[W]e have learning communities so that people get a sense of what's happening and how they can get their voice heard . . . . Through that process, you get more buy-in with teachers. And I think that they feel, then, that it's more valuable to them and their students, which I know I've already felt."

Although our researchers found teacher resistance to STARS in almost every school we visited, including a sizable minority who voiced a preference for the simplicity of a state test, teacher commitment was increasing slowly but surely in most schools.[5] It was not uncommon to hear testimony like this from teachers: "It has been a really unique situation to be part of, to see the attitudes of the teachers here change. There is something that they all have in common now. There is something that they are all working on and towards now and it is a source of real pride." Certainly, some of those who were on board were so because they felt they had no other choice: STARS was here to stay. But we also found a growing sense that STARS was the right thing to do:

> I would have said, six years ago—I did say six years ago when I moved here [from Texas]—"Why do we have to do all this? Why don't we just give a state test?" . . . Now, six years later, I've taken a change because I've seen what kind of information you can gain

from tests that are written to your curricula, that you have written and that the teachers have said is important to them.... If you can take this information that we're getting based on our test, on our kids, and use it wisely, that it is the way to go. And I wouldn't want to be in any other state right now, even though it's a lot of work. I would not want to be in any other state right now.[6]

Similarly, a superintendent told a story about two teachers who gave a report on curriculum and assessment to the local school board. He explained:

Our board was just amazed to see how impassioned our teachers are. They were like, "Man, if I wasn't sitting here, I would have never believed that those two teachers, specifically, could get that excited about curriculum and assessment." And it's been awesome to watch that take place. I mean you just don't mess with our teachers when it comes to this right now.

When teachers commit to creating school cultures of continuous improvement, they tend to exert considerable pressure on their colleagues to make the same commitment. In most of the schools we visited, for example, if a teacher was not focused on teaching and learning—if, for instance, he protected his pet projects irrespective of his students' needs—then he was perceived as unprofessional. Teachers talked about the need to "reassess what [we] are doing," to "look at ourselves with a more critical eye," and to "constantly assess and evaluate and to improve and change"—all in the name of avoiding complacency, because *that's what professionals do*. This kind of pressure to behave professionally is more powerful and sustaining than anything compliance could leverage.

When schools lack a critical core of teachers who place this kind of pressure on their peers, of course, it is difficult to move a staff to pull in the same direction. We did visit some schools that lacked a shared sense of purpose and professionalism, and while we might have found in them a heroic individual or two who labored to engender intense professional conversations, those conversations had little chance of taking root in this infertile ground. In a school in which the prevailing ethos continues to be "Why can't they just leave us alone?" even initiating these conversations is nearly impossible. This is the case as well in schools and districts that have placed the onus of standards and accountability on the shoulders of those teachers whose assessment data are reported to the state. Before those conversations can become meaningful—and before teachers will *perceive* them as meaningful—the school culture must support the notion that school improvement is *everyone's* responsibility. When that does happen— when all teachers feel themselves to be an important part of a shared mission of a school—professional development becomes not an event, a burden, or an opportunity, but rather a way of life in schools.

Building Data-Informed Professional Development Programs

This way of life is characterized by focused, critical, and collective examinations of teaching and learning. In the schools where we observed this way of life, these examinations were regularly informed by assessment data, which were often (literally) on the table as teams of teachers collectively made decisions about curriculum, instruction, and school improvement.[7] In some schools, data retreats were organized to determine how best to use the data to make curricular and instructional decisions; in others, this work was carried out in learning teams or department meetings. In any case, because assessment was viewed as *part of* teaching and learning, drawing inferences from data was a routine part of many teachers' work.

Perhaps because educators are not traditionally trained to do this work, and perhaps because this was the first time around, many schools ended up collecting more data than they needed—certainly more than they knew what to do with. They were, to use Roland S. Barth's phrase, "information rich and experience poor" (2001, 40). Educators in these schools were likely to perceive their work as "data driven," but the welter of data only drove them to distraction; they were, as we heard many times, "overwhelmed." They talked (sometimes, it seemed, obsessively) about "the numbers," but they had little capacity to draw the story from the data: to connect them to the kids and to the real-life decisions that happen in classrooms every day. The state and districts are developing tools and training for understanding and using data, but serious needs remain in this area.

Still, within these limitations, and with the assistance of the state and regional educational service units, Nebraska educators were learning to interpret and use data in their classrooms and curricula. They were disaggregating data by student groups, identifying achievement gaps as well as strengths and weaknesses in student performance, and evaluating the effectiveness of specific programs and strategies. Some were able to walk our researchers through a very specific rendering of their results—sometimes with the help of spreadsheets or "talking points" they had prepared—going back several years, identifying specific areas in which their students performed well at particular grade levels and others in which students struggled.

Mostly, teachers and administrators used assessment data to plan students' learning. But many also used that data to plan *teachers'* learning: to design *programs* of professional development, including targeted workshops, learning team meetings, and the like. In these schools, professional development became one part of an overarching school improvement effort; like curriculum and instruction, professional development was informed by what the school learned from assessment. This was common at the district level as well; one district, for instance, found that its high-poverty students were struggling, and so it designed a coordinated series of opportunities for teachers to learn more about working with these students. As commonsensical as it sounds, building a coordinated program of professional development around what educators learn from assessment data remains a rarity in U.S. schools today (Elmore 2004).

Designing Collaborative Structures and Strategies

These professional development programs rest on structures and strategies that promote collaboration among Nebraska educators. The overarching structure for these programs might be described as bottom-up, inverting the traditional model of professional development and disrupting traditional staff hierarchies. As one principal told us, "rather than everything coming down from the administration that this is how we need to do that, this is coming from the other direction, where teachers get together and talk about areas that need improve[ment]." In fact, in school after school, we heard administrators describe this same inversion. Here's a superintendent in another district:

> Instead of [administrators] giving [teachers] the information...we let them evaluate the data. So, somewhere in September, beginning of October, each department makes a report to the whole school staff: "This is the data from this year. We're really pleased with this. We really think we need to work on this. This will be part of our building action plan." And then each department writes a piece to the building action plan. We set a goal as a [district], based upon their data [and] teacher observation.

It was not uncommon to hear processes like these described as backwards—or, as one principal colorfully put it, "bass-ackwards." But as this principal insisted, the idea is that "the people that are closest to the students need to drive...instruction, and instruction will improve." So teachers, working collaboratively, were the primary force behind the school improvement process in these schools.

Within this bottom-up structure, schools employ a variety of professional development strategies to initiate and sustain collaboration among teachers. These range from informal grade-level and content-area meetings and common planning times to highly evolved, protocol-driven learning team sessions or curriculum mapping. But whatever specific strategies are employed, the purposes are the same: to share information, to plan curriculum and instruction together, to hone teachers' professional judgment, and generally to stay connected to and in conversation with one another.

Once again, these strategies mark a larger cultural shift in schools toward collective ownership of teaching and learning. Not only are teachers coming out of private practice, but so too are administrators. What's more, they're doing so in a way that recognizes the centrality of teacher expertise in school improvement. This is a major change in role for building and district administrators, who traditionally were trained as managers, not as facilitators of learning.[8] But instead of merely arranging and making a brief appearance at a professional development event, administrators in many schools have begun to come to the table as partners in promoting school improvement, as this high school principal describes:

> It is great to see teachers and administrators sitting around a table and we forget...their titles. That we are all looking at what's best for the kids. And it's taking different perspectives: administrators bring the leadership and the administrative perspective when the teachers bring the classroom and the one-on-one relationship that they have with those kids, and then all of that can be brought together to create something that is beneficial to all.

In order for this cultural shift even to begin, educators told us, *trust* must be established among colleagues. This often begins with administrators. Consider how this sixth-grade teacher (also a school assessment coordinator) explains the message teachers receive from administration: "They know that if they find a piece that isn't still working for them, it's not something they need to hide or be scared to share; it's something they can actually walk into [the principal's] office and say, 'All right, we're still not reaching where we need to . . . and we're using what we have to the fullest of our abilities. Do you have instructional strategies that we can use? Do you know of training we can go to?'" This is a large elementary school located in an urban area with high poverty and student diversity. As the educators in this school insisted, the scale and demographic challenges they faced made teacher collaboration all the more imperative. Indeed, it was routine in this school for teachers to visit each other's classrooms. They had a "permanent peer coach" who floated throughout the building, releasing teachers to observe each other. It took some time for teachers to become accustomed to this, but as the principal explained, now "it just happens all the time." Besides, he added, "a teacher watching another teacher teach is going to see some great benefits, more than having a conversation with me about an appraisal of teaching. They just take away ideas all the time when they watch somebody else teach . . . there's that dialogue that occurs."

But then consider another school. It's a middle school, but in almost every other way, it resembles the elementary school just discussed. It is large and located in another diverse, high-poverty, urban area. It has strong building leadership and capable teachers. It is located in a district that touts teamwork among teachers. But the district that houses this second school is different in this way: it provides rewards and punishments for teachers based on students' scores on district criterion-referenced tests. This makes it very difficult for the faculty of the school—though they are affable enough—to form truly *collegial* relationships in which they feel free to support *and* critique each other's and their own practice. When we conducted a focus group interview with four language arts teachers we witnessed congeniality, but also a palpable guardedness. At one point in the interview, one teacher said the following of a colleague who was in the room: "J. is a wonderful teacher. She is awesome, and I don't want her to see what I do in the classroom. It's embarrassing. It's really humiliating. . . . Nobody knows your IQ. Why is it I have to share my kids' scores with the whole world?" This kind of defensiveness is reasonable, given the cold calculus at play in this district. But it means that this teacher's interactions with her fellow teachers, though congenial, will not be truly collegial. Even when these teachers share students, they jealously protect those students' assessment results as theirs.[9]

Perhaps this dynamic explains Shirley Hord's finding that the fifth characteristic of professional learning communities—sharing teaching practice—is relatively rare in schools (2004, 1). Even in schools in which Hord and her colleagues found significant evidence of the other four characteristics—supportive and shared leadership, shared values and vision, collective learning and application of that learning, and supportive conditions—"the powerful, multiple, and entrenched barriers to *shared personal practice* remained virtually unmoved after 3 years of effort . . . Teachers did not visit one another's classrooms, collaboratively review student work, or engage in significant critical feedback with their colleagues" (Capers 2004, 152). Coming out of private practice means exposing one's work to the world; as the teacher in the second school discussed previously suggests, it's potentially humiliating and embarrassing.

But while sharing personal practice is surely never easy, it is made more so in school cultures in which teachers are partners, not competitors. Sadly, the focus of much discussion of assessment these days—including "value-added" assessment—is its alleged ability to shine a spotlight on individual teacher effectiveness. On the other hand, the still-emerging literature on collaborative teacher inquiry clearly indicates that when teachers learn, students learn. Whether those teachers use the critical friends approach, teacher research protocols, the teachers-teaching teachers model of the National Writing Project, "looking at student work" or lesson study strategies, or professional learning communities, teacher collaboration can be a powerful force for student learning and school improvement.[10] Therefore, measuring individual teachers' effectiveness and using those measurements to reward and punish teachers—no matter how sensitive the instrument—is not the way to improve schools. Instead, educational policy and practice must encourage teachers to collectively shed much-needed light on their shared practice and learn together how best to serve children. Papillion-La Vista schools, the subject of the next section, show what this kind of engaged and engaging professional development looks like.[11]

Creating New Models of Professional Development: Portrait of Practice

Compare this scene with the one with which I opened this chapter:

The cafeteria hums with unfocused early-morning energy. Teachers fall comfortably into and out of pairs and groups, saying hello, patting each other on the back, reaching for donuts and coffee at the table set up in the middle of the large room, picking up threads of conversations begun yesterday or before that.

After ten minutes or so, as if guided by an invisible hand, the teachers begin moving to tables, which are set up in rounds. A few straggle, standing in small circles, apparently oblivious to what goes on around them. But soon, the stragglers are good-naturedly called out—"Hey, don't you have somewhere to be?"—and they too find their places. It is time to work.

All at once, the tables are covered as folders, papers, pencils and pens, and laptops are unloaded from full arms and shoulder bags. The conversations find and settle into their table-level pitches and tones.

From several tables: "Who wants to start?"

And then: "Who's taking notes this time?"

At one table, Marie begins. Dave takes notes. Marie describes a poetry assessment she has designed. She explains that her goal is twofold: she wants students to have some language in their heads to describe what poems are doing, and she wants them to be familiar with the terms that the AP exam will use.

"Those are both important to these kids," Jean offers.

Marie agrees, but says she isn't happy with her kids' performance.

The table is suddenly abuzz with questions: "Are they getting caught up on the same terms, or different ones?" "How did they do compared to last year's group?" "Are the girls performing differently than the boys?" "What strategies have you used to teach the terms?" "Are these strategies different from the ones you've used in the past?" "Is the format of the test different this time?" "Do they use the terms in class, when they analyze poems?"

Several questions prompt brief discussion. The one about last year's group, for example, leads to a collective assessment of how last year's seniors compare with this year's. The question about gender prompts a discussion about how girls and boys are performing differently in math and physical education this year. At several points, team members offer a tentative "What if you tried...?" Meanwhile, Dave scribbles away.

After about fifteen minutes, Jean—the table leader—sums up: "Well, it sounds like you have some work to do and some ideas for how to do it. You're doing a great job. They're having a tough time with this one thing, but like we said last time, they are getting stronger overall."

Marie smiles, nods. She says she has some ideas for how to "go at this again." She thanks the group.

Dave hands Marie the sheet of notes and says, "I'll go next."

Although this scene unfolded one beautiful, cool April morning at Papillion-La Vista (Nebraska) High School, it could have taken place any month in any of that district's sixteen buildings. Papillion-

La Vista Public Schools (PLV) serves a fast-growing suburban community with approximately thirty-five-thousand residents and has added several schools in the last decade. Even as it has grown, however, the district has kept its focus on classroom-based assessments; indeed, it continues to use *only* classroom-based assessment for state reporting. And the results have been stellar; PLV consistently garners high ratings from the state on both assessment quality and student performance.

Jef Johnston, assistant superintendent of PLV, describes the genesis of his district's ambitious effort to include all teachers in its school improvement process:

> We started redesigning our curriculum in '99–'00....We formed a kind of think-tank with a couple dozen principals and teachers, and our early idea was to create teacher-friendly documents that merged curriculum, instruction, and assessment. We also started using teams to develop it all, because we figured the best way to make it meaningful to 700 educators was to involve them in development. Our perceived need was simply to do... better if we really wanted to help our children. At the time, I really wondered if the idea was too grand to carry out. Five years later, we have made more progress than I ever dreamed possible. (personal communication, 12/29/05)

According to Johnston, PLV's ultimate goal was K–12 integration, and for that to happen, all teachers would need to be involved. So the initial planning team set up pilot teams of four teachers from each level: elementary school, middle school, and high school. These teams piloted the process that would eventually become the Classroom Goals meetings. At the end of this first year, the administration decided to lengthen the school day by about ten minutes per day to allow one additional professional development day per month. The following year, every teacher in every building in PLV served on a learning team with three or four colleagues. The teams follow the same protocol as the pilots, with collective examination of student work at the center. Now in its third year, the learning team approach is popular among PLV teachers, 90 percent of whom indicated on an anonymous survey that it was a valuable process and should continue.

Laura Miller, Classroom Teacher, Papillion-La Vista Public Schools
Our Classroom Goals program, first implemented during the 2003–4 school year, brings teams of teachers together to collaborate on the

use of our classroom assessment data to drive instructional decisions. All teachers in the district meet monthly to share an assessment used to analyze students' strengths and weaknesses. During our meetings, we collaboratively develop instructional strategies designed to target student weaknesses and improve learning in our goal areas. The frequency of our monthly team meetings holds us accountable for implementing our instructional strategies in the classroom as we continually monitor student learning.

Classroom Goals teams consist of four to five teachers, and the diversity of our teams varies throughout the district, according to building and department needs. Some of our secondary teams meet by departments or as interdisciplinary groups, and some elementary teams meet as grade-level or vertical teams. Regardless of the various advantages of structuring the teams differently, by being a part of a consistent team all year, we build peer relationships while being accountable for taking active steps toward reaching our personal classroom goals.

In order to prepare for our first Classroom Goals meeting, we complete a background information form [see Figure 5–2], which guides us in communicating our learning targets and assessment results to our team. The process of preparing for Classroom Goals has taught us not only that we *should* analyze student strengths and weaknesses throughout assessment but also *how* to analyze those strengths and weaknesses. Furthermore, the process encourages us to be reflective and analytical about assessment all the time, not just when considering our present goal.

Our background information form, as well as other Classroom Goals documents, is a tool that effectively builds professional development and assessment literacy. It does this by communicating expectations. These expectations, such as providing students with timely and specific feedback, naturally become an appropriate discussion focus during our team meetings. Other Classroom Goals documents similarly guide us in developing our goals, documenting and graphing student progress, implementing specific instructional strategies, and reflecting on the results.

Being part of a Classroom Goals team builds positive school community and a culture of trust and support. Within our teams, it is safe to bring up areas of concern or professional struggles without the pressure of being evaluated or critiqued. For some of us, the change from working in isolation to working collaboratively has nudged us out of our comfort zones, but the benefits of being supported by a

Classroom Goals Form

Background Information

Date:_____   Teacher:_____

Complete this form prior to the first assessment.

What Assessment Method did you use?

___Selected Response   ___Essay

___Performance   ___ Personal Communication

What was the Purpose of the assessment?

___Diagnostic   ___To Adjust Instruction

___To Obtain a Grade

What was the Learning Target of the assessment?

Students will_____

- ◆ What strategies did you use to help your students succeed?
- ◆ Based on the results of the assessment, what are the strengths of the students?
- ◆ Based on the results of the assessment, what are the weaknesses of the students?
- ◆ Describe the feedback you gave to students after the assessment.

  For example: When did you give them feedback? What did students do as a result of the feedback? Did students know the criteria from a scoring guide? Did students get feedback from other students?

Please bring to the Classroom Goals meeting:

- ◆ Analyzing Student Strengths and Weaknesses form
- ◆ Six samples of student work, representing two high-scoring students, two middle-scoring students, and two low-scoring students

Figure 5–2 Classroom Goals Form

team soon ease the anxiety. Also, we experience positive professional peer pressure to try the instructional strategies suggested by our peers and prepare for our monthly meetings.

Overall, as teachers we appreciate having the time and structure for professional communication and collaboration. Furthermore, we value the choice we have in determining our own goals and are more personally invested in them as a result. Most of us agree that Classroom Goals is the preferred model for professional development because it directly relates *our* classrooms and *our* students' needs. It has proved to be a far more valuable use of our time than traditional professional development trainings that involved bringing in outside presenters. We have all gained more respect for the power of our collective expertise and the benefits it has on student learning.

Twenty-First-Century Professional Development

The false promise of the accountability agenda is that meaningful and sustainable reform is possible through *designing controls* rather than *developing capacity* (Darling-Hammond 1997). Not only is this bad educational policy; it is a bad way to conduct human relationships. As Deborah Meier has written, "It may be that the implicit denigration of the common-sense human judgment of the adults in kids' lives will be, in the long term, the greatest price paid in our current mania for high-stakes testing" (2002, 132).

From an engagement perspective, it is imperative that the adults with whom children spend a good part of their days are well-trained, active, trustworthy professionals—and are treated that way. No meaningful and sustainable school improvement is possible until we acknowledge and strengthen the connection between student and teacher learning. This is why next-generation professional development must embrace teacher learning not as a mark of deficiency, but as a mark of professionalism.

Actually, we already know—the professional development literature is quite clear on this—that the kind of inquiry-based, ongoing, embedded, professional learning for teachers that we see in Papillion-La Vista is a force for improved *student* learning. But because the accountability agenda has promoted a truncated view of teacher expertise—and has sometimes opposed that notion altogether—we have yet to muster the political will or educational imagination to put structures and systems in place to support the kind of professional development we know we need. The Nebraska Story, while incomplete, gives us a glimpse of what a statewide effort to build school capacity through teacher expertise and leadership might look like. It's true that Nebraska is not immune from the tendency of systemic reform processes to create insiders and outsiders (Corbett 2000; Elmore 2004); serious concerns remain in particular about those teachers who work in grades and content areas other than those whose results are reported to the state. But at their best, Nebraska educators show how teachers can begin to institutionalize and systematize professional development that is based on developing rich, collegial relationships and collective expertise

Notes

1. In addition, the law pushes states to ensure teacher competency in content areas via standardized tests. Nebraska has balked at this requirement, and this has caused the U.S. Department of Education to cite it as one of nine states in danger of losing federal funding for not making a sufficient effort to comply. However, at the time of this writing, no state has shown that it has a qualified teacher in every core classroom, as required by the law. See Feller (2006).

2. Although I'm wary of arguments that school cultures ought to be patterned after corporate cultures (see, for instance, Deal and Peterson 1999), it's worth noting that the business world, too, has acknowledged the inadequacies of traditional, passive, individualistic training. General Electric, Bell Labs, and other successful companies are famous for their collaborative, team-based, problem-solving, cross-departmental cultures of innovation.

3. In 2002, according to Director of Statewide Assessment Pat Roschewski, the responsibility to support learning teams was handed over to the seventeen regional educational service units across the state (personal correspondence, 5/11/06).

4. This literature mostly highlights single schools or districts. Although the Southwest Educational Development Laboratory (SEDL) builds *networks* of PLCs, these networks are not coordinated with state standards and assessment policies and practices. Indeed, the PLC literature rarely discusses assessment at all. When it does, it generally equates assessment with statewide tests, which are treated as obstacles to the kind of teacher and student learning being promoted. For example, Anita Pankake writes that at one high school in which she and her colleagues were trying to launch a learning community, students "take the state test required for graduation during their sophomore year; for the majority of students, that leaves 2 full academic years to learn and grow, free from state-wide

tests" (2004, 128). So the SEDL's PLC program takes root where state tests do not dominate—a move that both makes sense and severely limits the scope and impact of the PLCs.

5. A 2005 study by Boss et al. found that educators (teachers, principals, staff developers, and district assessment coordinators) who are involved in the STARS process generally have positive perceptions of STARS (Isernhagen 2005, 154).

6. An increasing number of educators in our study came to see themselves as standing *with* the state against what they perceived to be the encroachment of the federal government. This teacher captures the sentiment: "I'm not too excited about the possibility of... Mr. Bush coming in here and telling us how we need to assess our kids because what works in Texas may not work in Nebraska."

7. In some schools, teachers did the data analysis; in others, assessment coordinators or other staff analyzed the data and provided those analyses to teachers. Some administrators adamantly insisted that teachers should not be asked to do data analysis—to be "married to data," as one principal put it. In any event, in most Nebraska schools, teachers at least got help with data analysis.

8. Each of the Comprehensive Evaluation Project's reports includes studies of changes in administrators' roles and responsibilities under STARS. Beginning in 2004, the Nebraska Department of Education, in concert with the University of Nebraska-Lincoln, has increased its focus on building and district leadership, including a statewide leadership council and an administrators' version of the assessment leadership program described in Chapter 4.

9. This school touted itself as "collaborative," and the administration pointed to the amount of time staff spent together as evidence of that. But as Andy Hargreaves (1995) indicates, collaboration can be designed in ways that erode, rather than promote, collegial relationships. The potential dangers of collaboration are many: it can be administratively imposed and designed in ways that do not meet teachers' needs as learners; it can encourage narrow-minded "groupthink"; it can create small, elite groups of teachers in the know, which can erode staff morale in general; it can be used to denigrate or dismiss outright teachers' need for solitary reflection; it can lead to balkanization (the creation of insular groups within a school that do not communicate with one another) (Hargreaves 1995). All of these dangers must be anticipated and guarded against. The key response to most of them is to *involve teachers in the planning and execution of the professional development*. What is wanted here is professional development for teachers by teachers.

10. See Bambino (2002); Burney (2004); Fernande
    Gray (1986); Huffman and Hipp (2003); La
    Lieberman and Wood (2003); McDonald (2(
    Mohr et al. (2004); and Watanabe (2002).

11. As in other chapters, depictions that identify actual schoℴ
    are not drawn from Comprehensive Evaluation Project resea.
    rather from my own experiences and observations as an invited visitor ᴛᴏ
    these schools. In this instance, the description of the table-level conver-
    sation is a composite of several such conversations I witnessed at
    Papillion-La Vista High School. The names are pseudonyms.

Engaging 6 Community Members

Extending the Conversation

A warm spring evening, 7 o'clock.[1] The auditorium, filled almost to capacity, is stifling. Half of this town of one thousand people must be in attendance tonight.

This is not lost on the kindly principal, who graciously greets the audience and introduces the teachers and staff.

One of the teachers—Ms. B., poised, with a powerful voice and a pleasant demeanor—takes the microphone next and announces that the theme of the evening is storytelling. All the student projects to be shared this evening, she says, are a part of the history of the town, the story of its people. "Listen," she says, "and hear who we are."

"And," she adds, "these projects also meet state standards. We teachers will be happy to share with you the assessments we use to measure student learning."

With that, she turns over the stage to a group of elementary-aged students who (with a little help from their teacher) bravely squeak out the poetry of local writers and stutter through their research into the lives of town founders. They are followed by middle school students who proudly display the immigrant trunks they have made by hand, modeled on those of their nineteenth-century ancestors. They have filled their immigrant trunks with historical artifacts, each a prompt for a story from the past. Finally, high school students confidently share their historical and mathematical research into town weather patterns and recorded times at regional track meets.

Meanwhile, the audience—parents, local businesspeople and other community members, and assorted invited guests—are charmed, rapt, impressed. Mostly, they sit in silent wonder. But occasionally, they turn to a neighbor and whisper: "I could never have done that at that age," "That was my grandfather," "I didn't know that," or "Remind me to tell you about the time…"

When Ms. B. returns to the stage and asks the audience to give the kids one final hand, the applause is thunderous. Determined to demonstrate that its appreciation is more than ceremonial, the crowd rises as one and continues applauding far longer than decorum requires. Onstage, the kids bow awkwardly several times.

Several minutes pass before Ms. B. can be heard again. When the din settles, she asks audience members to turn to a partner and have a brief conversation about what they witnessed this evening. "Just share your reactions," she says, "or maybe tell a story of your own."

And they do: Pairs and small groups of people fall into easy conversation. They praise the kids' efforts, perhaps bragging just a little about their own child. They talk about what they learned: "I've lived here my whole life, and I never knew how that cemetery got started." And they tell their own stories: "That story reminded me of the time my grandmother..."

After ten or fifteen minutes, Ms. B. retakes the stage and notes that paper and pens are coming around. She would like everyone to write down three things: (1) one thing that you saw tonight that you liked, (2) one thing you saw tonight that made you wonder, and (3) one thing you wish you had seen tonight. She also invites the audience members to write any suggestions they have for the performance or for the projects. Teachers will be around to collect the papers and pens in a few minutes. Then the comments will be recorded and shared with the whole staff and the kids and used when they set school improvement goals.

"And please," Ms. B. adds, "come talk to us, or come see us, anytime. We'd love to have you, and we'd love to continue the conversations begun here tonight."

As people scribble away and hand their papers down the rows, Ms. B. leaves them with one final thought. "Knowing your history means knowing yourself," she says. "And knowing yourself—and in particular how your story intersects with the stories of others—is a key to living well.

"Know that," Ms. B. says, "and you know how to live well anywhere."

The moment Ms. B. concludes, everyone, all at once, is talking. Some are catching up, others trading impressions of the evening. But most, Ms. B. would be happy to know, are telling their own stories.

———————◦◦◦———————

PRINCIPAL:[2] We were doing lots of neat things. And I know that some of those things... they've already fallen by the wayside because it takes too much time to develop assessments to match those projects that kids were doing.... With all the testing that you have to do, we've lost some of that neat stuff we were doing getting kids into the community and community members into the school and working together on projects...It was just easier to drop some of that stuff and just do the assessments that they work on at the service unit.

INTERVIEWER: [So how do you work with the community now?]

PRINCIPAL: Just this last week, Wednesday, we spent an hour and a half, probably, talking to board members about assessments and STARS and all that because we have, like, six new board members and they needed to be briefed. So, we spent quite a bit of time at our retreat telling them about assessments, telling them about STARS and what we do with it, and the information we have to put together. We talked about the [District Assessment] Portfolio. We talked about the data, keeping the data. We talked about reliability and cut scores and all of that stuff.

Engaging School-Community Relationships

Although these two schools are illustrative of very different approaches to school-community relations, of course it would not be fair to judge them based only on these isolated bits of evidence. True, in the latter case, the technical discourse of assessment has narrowed—in a particularly heartbreaking way—both what the school does in and with the community and how its educators talk about their work. But as we learned when we visited, not all teachers *have* let go of those community-based projects, and the light of learning is hardly snuffed out in this school. And true, in the former case, the display of student work was powerful. But the kinds of conversations that emerge from the public sharing of student work are rarely as warm and fuzzy as this celebratory scene might suggest.

Indeed, school-community relationships are never easy or painless. Certainly, they should celebrate student, teacher, and school success whenever and wherever it is found, but in a democratic society, a public school that dares to build strong ties with its public invites the clashing of deeply held values, beliefs, and ideas. Ask any room of people what constitutes student, teacher, or school success in the first place, and you are likely to receive many different and conflicting answers. But probing, candid public deliberation on questions like these—*engagement*, in the sense of confronting or taking on—*is* the work of "workshops of democracy" (Bracey 2002, 104).

Unfortunately, however, there seems to be widespread consensus that public schools and their public are only moving apart. A decade of Kettering Foundation research revealed in 1996 that although the majority of Americans look favorably on their local schools—a

consistent finding of annual Phi Delta Kappa/Gallup polls, as well—
we have seen at the same time "an erosion of the historic commitment to the idea of schools for the benefit of the entire community"
(Mathews 1996, 2). Kettering researcher David Mathews identified
several reasons for this erosion, including market-based reforms,
increasing financial control by state governments, professionally set
standards, poor communication by administrators, educators' lack of
responsiveness to parents' concerns, and so on (2–4). But above all,
claims Mathews, the culprit is an impoverished public life. His
provocative thesis is that there is no public for public schools (3).

   To be sure, it is easy to agree with Mathews that our public life is
in many ways wanting.[3] And the literature on school-community partnerships seems to support his contention that social developments are
to blame for the drift between schools and communities; here, we find
much discussion of a felt loss of communal life, increased time pressures owing to developments such as the increase in single-parent
households, the relatively low percentage of households with school-
aged children as baby boomers age, communication difficulties in
communities with rapidly changing demographics, and so on (see, for
example, Chadwick 2004; Cunningham 2003; Decker and Decker
2003; Dodd and Konzal 2002; Epstein et al. 1997; and Sanders 2006).
But while each of these developments likely has some impact on the
drift, we need to confront the fact that over the past twenty-five years,
*the accountability agenda has taken the schools away from their communi-
ties*. Again and again, communities are told that schools cannot be
trusted, educators are not doing their jobs, and their children are not
competitive in the global marketplace. Rolling back a well-established
tradition of local control in American education, the accountability
agenda has retooled schools to be responsive to special— especially
business—interests, rather than to the public good (Bracey 2002;
Cunningham 2003; Clinchy 2004; Emery and Ohanian 2004).

   Of course, accountability schemes like No Child Left Behind are
promoted as serving community, or at least parental, interests because
they allegedly give them information they need to make good
"choices" for kids. (I'll return to the reason for those scare quotes in a
moment.) But, as Deborah Meier remarks, "NCLB assumes that neither children, their families, nor their communities can be trusted to
make important decisions about their schools" (2004, 71). Instead, in
the name of preparing students for a globalized, migratory, urbanized
world, the accountability agenda insists that community—the environment, the landscape, the social network in which a child lives—

does not matter. Because accountability hawks conflate equity with uniformity, they promote a placelessness: a one-size-fits-all, context-be-damned, teacher-proof approach to education that disempowers communities by effectively making them irrelevant. If kids in New York City or Fairbanks, Alaska, should know and do the same things at the same time as kids in Winnebago, Nebraska, what does it matter that those kids in Winnebago live on an economically impoverished but culturally rich Native American reservation? Context doesn't count; only results count. And anything other than standardized education amounts to provincialism and cheats kids of the opportunity to compete in the global marketplace.

Meanwhile, of course, those results—expressed, always, in terms of easily digested numbers—lead many educators to treat accountability as a public relations game and to engage their communities, if at all, only when it is time to explain (and perhaps defend) their numbers, their public rankings, and their Adequate Yearly Progress status. Administrators may get called before their boards or be contacted by the media for damage control, but beyond that, educators have every reason to keep their heads low. By fostering distrust between educators and community members, then, the accountability agenda impoverishes school-community relationships.

The truth is, the drift between communities and schools is no accident; it's the result of a calculated wedge-driving campaign, a key component of the accountability agenda. NCLB begins with the premise that schools are deficient and its primary function is to expose those deficiencies in the name of parental choice. The U.S. Department of Education's NCLB website is unambiguous on this point (www.ed.gov/nclb). A page titled "Helping Families by Supporting and Expanding Choice," for example, indicates that NCLB is about "empowering parents with information" and includes discussion of public school choice, supplemental educational services, charter schools, magnet schools, the Voluntary School Choice Program, the D.C. School Choice Initiative, and scholarships for kids in schools identified as "in need of improvement." The page "School Choices for Parents" provides information on some of these same topics—plus private schools and home schools. Currently, NCLB provides publicly funded choice only for public schools (an early version of NCLB included provisions for private school choice, but it was pulled before passage of the bill). But as we move closer to the "sword of Damocles" year 2014, and states and schools continue not to measure up to the requirements of the law, suspicion grows that the true end game of NCLB is the dismantling of public education in favor of privatization.[4]

In any event, NCLB maintains a laserlike focus on rooting out schools' deficiencies, rather than *supporting* rich, engaged school-community relations to improve all schools. (Indeed, one searches in vain through the NCLB website for any discussion of communities.) Of course, this emphasis is consistent with accountability logic; the purpose is to provide information on an investment, much like companies report to their stockholders. And if the company isn't performing—well, then it may be time to restructure the portfolio. The market determines winners and losers.

But importantly, the kind of information proffered by NCLB's approach to accountability is not the kind the public says it wants or needs. The four-year National Dialogue project run by Mid-continent Research for Education and Learning (McREL) found that merely reporting tests scores, as NCLB calls for, "does not answer the questions parents truly care about when it comes to their own children's performance or the performance of the schools their children attend" (Lefkowits and Miller 2006, 405).[5] And yet, because so much rides on those test scores, educators find themselves spending endless hours parsing charts and graphs with parents and other community members rather than sharing their observations, stories, and professional judgments about children. This chartspeak will hardly help educators and community members listen across and engage differences, which is precisely what schools and communities, especially in diverse or diversifying areas, need most. Of course, data about school and student performance are not meaningless to parents and other community members. And of course some educators and schools need to do a better job and that should be known. But when educators are fixed on tending the machinery of accountability rather than tending to the humanity of children, it is impossible to build those messy, human relationships that are the lifeblood of diverse democracy.

But we need not make this point so abstractly: We know that school-community partnerships are an effective tool for school improvement. The benefits of school-community partnerships are well documented; they include increased student achievement (especially for poor and minority students), better student attendance, better homework habits, better student attitudes and behaviors, higher teacher morale and decreased teacher turnover, improved school climate, higher trust in educators, more public support for school funding, and more (Chadwick 2004; Cunningham 2003; Decker and

Decker 2003; Dodd and Konzal 2002; Epstein et al. 1997; Sanders 2006). Notice that the relational benefits—what we might think of as the building blocks of good relationships, such as morale and trust—sit side by side with accountability hawks' prized outcomes, especially student achievement. Put simply, schools work better and students learn better when kids and adults work together.

The literature on school-community partnerships is bursting with innovative ideas; a small sample would include family resource centers, community food banks, student-led conferences, community readers' theater or read-alouds, family journal writing, family writing groups or workshops, storytelling festivals, arts and crafts workshops, community science fairs, service learning and entrepreneurship programs, student-parent-teacher advisory councils, family math nights, English language learners classes for parents and community members, parent-teacher action research, community garden clubs, and after-school tutoring programs. Readers of the literature will find useful conceptual tools for imagining the work of partnering—Joyce Epstein's six types of involvement (parenting, communicating, volunteering, learning at home, decision-making, collaborating with community), for instance (Epstein et al. 1997).[6] They will also find advice, tips, examples, and overviews of relevant research (Chadwick 2004, Decker and Decker 2003, Epstein et al. 1997, Sanders 2006, and all practical handbooks or sourcebooks.[7]). Readers who spend any time with this material will soon come to recognize key ingredients in effective school-community partnerships, such as communication, trust, respect (for each other, for diversity), motivation, shared visions or purposes and goals, flexibility, patience, and so on.

But these readers will come to see as well that there is no magic formula, no secret recipe for these partnerships. And building and sustaining them is more complex than simply creating more and more opportunities and trying to involve parents and community members in everything all at once. School-community relationships are always and irreducibly context dependent. Because every school, every group of parents, and every community is different, forging meaningful and lasting partnerships in each context is necessarily a unique experience.

And this is precisely why Nebraska has built, with STARS, a state system of *local* assessments. In Chapter 3, I described a rich tradition of close ties between Nebraska schools and communities. Many Nebraska educators view their communities as learning labs. Students in Palmer, Nebraska, work with local community members on a community math program; students in Cedar Bluffs participate in an interdisciplinary study (history, science, writing) of the Platte River, which runs through their town; students in Heartland Community Schools conduct oral and archival history on their towns; students in Wayne participate in a creative writing journal exchange with community members; students in Rising City write alongside adults in their community in a journal project devoted to public deliberation on the fate of a struggling school.[8] Educators in these communities believe that place-conscious, community-based learning can help students live well *anywhere*—precisely because it engages them in the real work of democracy: working on and working out public problems.

Several of the projects just mentioned are affiliated with the Nebraska Writing Project and its successful Rural Voices, Country Schools (RVCS) program, which aims to strengthen ties between schools and communities in rural areas. Robert E. Brooke, director of the Nebraska Writing Project, suggests that the RVCS program operates on the premise that "real accountability develops when students and teachers engage with the local and regional communities who sponsor them" (2003a, ix). Brooke and his colleague Carol MacDaniels (2003) go on to suggest that "Nebraska is attempting to implement a version of place-conscious education in the very design of its assessment process" (170). In other words, instead of requiring all students to know, do, and be tested on the same things at the same time, Nebraska has built a system that is responsive to the needs, strengths, and character of its communities—whether rural, suburban, or urban.

At a 2001 press conference, Nebraska commissioner of education Douglas Christensen (2001b) explained why he believed it was so important to keep education in the hands of local educators: "Informed conversations, and informed decisions, are the heart and soul of democracy." STARS, he said, is intended to be a tool to prompt local conversations about education and its place in each Nebraska community. At the state level, the Nebraska Department of Education has modeled this practice by sponsoring deliberative conversations such as a series of "public policy forums" in which a wide range of educational partners—teachers, administrators, staff developers, higher education representatives, local and state board members, legislators and policymakers, parents, and other community members—gather to explore questions such as How do we use data to energize the school improvement process? and What do we need to engage all of the stakeholders in the school improvement process? But finally, it is those local conversations, Commissioner Christensen and his staff insist, that will make a difference for Nebraska schools and communities.

Unlike NCLB, STARS aims to do more than pin scarlet letters—INOI for in need of improvement, for instance—to the breasts of schools in order to shame them into getting better. Rather, it operates on the premise that *all* schools should improve, from wherever they are and under their unique circumstances. This is why the commissioner has insisted repeatedly that rank-ordering schools undermines the goals of STARS. Such comparisons not only are "inherently unfair," as noted psychometrician Robert Linn (2000) has suggested, but also prompt educators to compete with each other for position, rather than compete with themselves for sustained, meaningful improvement (see Roschewski 2003). And so, STARS provides more than a set of test scores. Its annual *State of the Schools Report* is a rich compendium of school data (see www.nde.state.ne.us). It includes information about student performance, assessment quality, and student and teacher demographics. This allows the reader to place school results in context, including how the school is changing from year to year. What it does not allow the reader to do—to the chagrin of some local media—is draw easy comparisons between and among schools and districts.

As we'll see, not all Nebraska schools and districts are using STARS as a tool for prompting community conversations; indeed, in some communities, it has had precisely the chilling effect on school-community relationships that accountability regimes have had elsewhere in the country. Of all the ambitious goals of STARS, this is the one on which Nebraskans have the most work to do. The state and its districts need to do more at the policy and practice levels to promote meaningful and sustainable school-community partnerships. Nevertheless, STARS remains the only state standards and assessment system that recognizes and preserves local control of and responsibility for curriculum, instruction, and assessment with the aim of preserving and enhancing school-community relationships. For that reason alone—at least from an engagement perspective—it is well worth watching (see Figure 6–1).

School-Community Relationships in Nebraska

In previous chapters, I identified cultural shifts in Nebraska schools and then described trends within those shifts. Here, it would be an overstatement to say that our researchers observed a cultural shift toward the kind of engaged school-community relationships outlined earlier. For the most part, public engagement (to use the piece of jargon most in favor at the moment) remains in most Nebraska

Two Views of School-Community Relationships	
Accountability	**Engagement**
Unearned distrust	Earned trust
Investment audit	Conversation
Transaction	Interaction
Public relations	Public involvement
Placelessness	Place consciousness
Competition	Continuous improvement
Infrequent	Ongoing

Figure 6–1 Two Views of School-Community Relationships

schools a challenge, an as-yet-unrealized goal. To be sure, a handful have strengthened community ties through the STARS process (as we'll see), and a few have restricted or severed those ties. But in general, Nebraska teachers and administrators do not believe school-community relationships, to date, have been altered dramatically as a result of STARS. They do not give themselves very high marks even for communicating effectively with parents and community members, never mind involving them in school improvement efforts. Although we did not find the kind of fear and loathing of meddlesome parents and other community members that teachers are often charged with harboring, educators did often talk about their parents and communities as generally "apathetic."

Still, educators in our study schools demonstrated a deep commitment to building strong school-community relationships. Although many administrators in particular expressed serious worries about their ability to arouse among community members an active interest in the schools, almost every one of our study schools had set public engagement as a high priority for the near future. Many schools were devising specific strategies and plans for that purpose.

Clearly, as a state, Nebraska is not where it wants to be in terms of fostering strong school-community relationships. But we were able to identify some trends in Nebraska schools that are worth watching.

Getting the House in Order

Educators in almost every Nebraska school we visited voiced dissatisfaction with their relationships with parents and other community members. In many cases, they felt this was simply a time issue. One school administrator told us, "We haven't done a good job of reaching out to [the community]. We've been so involved in the process right here and the sense of urgency we've had to do [and do and do] that we haven't had time." Educators in this situation foresaw a time when their process would be reliable enough that their workload would ease—but they weren't there yet.

Educators in other schools had made a conscious decision not to "extend the conversation" until they were confident that everyone *inside* the school was comfortable with it. "We felt that what we needed to do was start with our staff first," another building administrator explained to us, "so that they have complete understanding so that they could go out into the community and talk intelligently about what it is that we are doing and why we are doing it." Teachers, too, talked about learning the local assessment system, and becoming familiar with the process, before feeling comfortable sharing it with people outside the schools. These educators envisaged strong internal relationships as a foundation for strong external ones. They were mindful that they couldn't "do everything at once" and they didn't want to push the process. "We're just not there yet," we heard more than once.

There is some support for this cautious, deliberate, inside-out approach in school reform research. Richard Elmore, for instance, has written about the need for educators to develop strong relationships of responsibility and shared commitment internally before "external accountability" is likely to have a positive effect (2004, 114). Ambitious school reformers—many of them with an eye on their resumes and their political legacies—are likely to be impatient with this slow, deliberate process. And certainly there is some political risk in delaying the expanded conversation. But these Nebraska teachers and administrators insist that it takes time to develop the kind of relationships on which meaningful school improvement programs can be built.

Using a New Language to Communicate with Parents and Community Members

But even if educators wish to slow down or delay these community conversations, they are at least beginning to happen, thanks, in part, to STARS. For the first time, the average Nebraska citizen has access to three kinds of information about each school in the state: student performance, assessment quality, and school and student characteristics. These data are not only new but also unconventional, and they require contextualization before they will make much sense. And so educators are more or less forced to communicate in new ways with their communities.

Take, for example, the issue of comparing and ranking schools. As many teachers and administrators told us, the public and (especially) the media are susceptible to what journalist Peter Sacks calls "the powerful elegance of a single number" (1999, 69). Who's on top? Who's at the bottom? How can we quantify the schools' performance? A small minority of educators we visited viewed this mentality as so deeply bred into the American psyche that the state might as well give in to a state test and at least "compare apples to apples." But most had committed themselves to educating parents and other community members about how to read and respond to STARS data, and, in particular, the dangers of comparing and ranking schools. Several, like this district assessment coordinator, talked about "changing the question": "[W]e have four elementary schools and we don't compare and say, 'Well, this elementary school is doing better than this.' We say, 'How have you helped the kids grow?'" In fact, none of our study schools used data to compare schools within a district or to compare themselves with other schools elsewhere in the state—though several educators noted that the media (especially local newspapers) were quick to make such comparisons. As one assessment coordinator told us, educators "try to approach [STARS as] a good opportunity for us to see what students are doing and learn how to improve the learning opportunities for all these kids and try not to point fingers and compare between districts or between classrooms, between teachers. But you know that gets done." The point, as a superintendent put it, is not to rank-order schools, teachers, or kids, but rather to ensure that "we all improve."

The multiple kinds of data provided by STARS allow educators to shape their message in richly contextual ways. They can talk not only about student performance but also about how they assessed that performance and the school factors that shape the school's particular challenges and strengths. Several teachers and administrators told us about using STARS and their local assessment process as an opportunity to talk with parents and other community members about *why* they were doing what they were doing; assessment language itself, in many cases, provided focus for these conversations.[9] A building administrator explained to us that STARS "has been good because we actually can sit down with parents and say, 'Here's the standards; here is where your child is; this is how far your child needs to advance by the time they graduate... It's right there in front of them and they can see it, so I think it has been good. The parents appreciate it." We heard the same idea from many teachers, who told us that standards and assessment open up "a channel" with parents. For example, a high school math teacher said, "It has provided good feedback for parent-teacher conferences. You can say, 'This is what the student had to do, this is what they have done, this is what they have yet to learn.'"

Teachers in several schools talked about using assessment data as evidence to support their professional judgment; as a fifth-grade teacher told us, "you can put the [assessment results] in front of the parents and say, 'You know, your student is struggling or your student is doing well, and here is the test result and that backs up what I see in the classroom.'" For these teachers, as a high school language arts teacher in another district put it, assessment "helps us to be more professional. Teachers are sometimes not regarded too highly and I think this gives us a way to say, 'But look, we do very good work,' and that is very important."

While our researchers observed a clear trend in Nebraska schools toward using standards and assessment as a tool for increasing communication with community members, especially parents, several schools in our study viewed school-community communication as their major struggle. In some cases, educators' efforts to educate their community about STARS were being undermined by the determination of local media to reduce standards and assessment to a numbers game. In others, rapidly changing community demographics, usually owing to the growth of immigrant and refugee populations, presented challenges to communication.[10] This was especially the case in the Nebraska communities that were seeing large influxes of Latinos, many of whom did not speak English. These schools were developing communication channels—from writing bilingual newsletters to participating in the start-up of Spanish newspapers—but they had considerable work to do to reach these families.

Moving (Slowly) Toward Involving Community Members in School Improvement

While we observed modest growth in Nebraska schools' communication with their communities, only a few of our study schools had implemented programs or processes that ensured significant, meaningful community involvement in the school improvement process—though, again, many had set this goal. However, we did spend time in several schools that had recently begun to move in this direction. Recall, for instance, Mr. Sands and his school from Chapter 2. This was a small, K–12 school on a Native American reservation. They had instituted public reviews of student graduation portfolios that included "significant members of the community," such as parents and tribal elders. Mr. Sands explained that the craftsmanship of the portfolios and the public sharing were a "mark of the people who live here"—people, he said, who didn't value test scores, but instead wanted to be shown what students could do. The portfolio review—during which the invited guests evaluated the student work alongside teachers—was part of a larger effort to connect the school's work to cultural traditions and values. The goal: to help the students value their community and its culture and to help the community value the students and the school. For Mr. Sands and his staff, school improvement involved bringing together the resources of the school and the community.

This kind of community involvement is not altogether unusual in smaller Nebraska towns, where there is a long tradition of close school-community ties.[11] Among our study schools, large, urban districts had fewer such projects and were far more likely to use standardized, criterion-referenced tests. But that does not mean they were not working toward school-community collaboration. One large urban middle school, for instance, had developed a number of initiatives with this end in view, including a school improvement team that included several parents and community members, a family liaison on staff, after-school tutoring by teachers and community members, and a robust parent volunteer program that logged approximately two thousand hours each school year. The school principal explained that parents "may not always agree with us, but they are very supportive." Why? In large part because the school door was open to them—"they're in our school all the time"—and they felt as though their voices were heard in the school. This is not to say that parents continually interfered with the staff. To the contrary, they functioned as a kind of extended support staff, reading with students in special education classrooms, assisting them in computer labs, tutoring them after school, putting up and taking down bulletin boards, helping teachers prepare their rooms for the first day of school, attending field trips, and the like. And their participation was designed by the teachers; as they explored their school improvement goals, each content-area team was asked, "How are you going to involve the home and the parents in the students' learning?"

A growing number of teachers in our study schools were using student work on assessments—essays written for the statewide writing assessment, for instance, or portfolios—to engage parents in conversation about their child's learning. This was particularly prevalent in the area of writing. Several teachers talked about sharing the Six Traits with parents in hopes they would "reinforce what students are trying to do at home." A fourth-grade teacher told us about sharing actual examples of students' writing with parents and asking the parents to use the language of the assessment to "make a judgment" about the writing. Doing this, she explained, helped parents gain a more concrete understanding of the teacher's goals as well as their child's performance.

Although teachers across the state had begun to put student work on the table during parent-teacher conferences—and some had moved to student-led conferences—few had found meaningful ways to *involve* parents in their child's learning or in the school improvement process more generally. And few schools had parlayed these nascent conversations into systematic community involvement programs. At present, though many educators across the state talk passionately about the need to do just that, only small steps have been taken in that direction.

Extending the Conversation: Portrait of Practice

Nebraska City, Nebraska,[12] is a small city—population 7,500—in the southeastern part of the state. While its overall population has been steady in recent years, its Latino population has increased dramatically. Arbor Day originated in this city, a fact of which its residents are proud. Indeed, the citizens of Nebraska City are mindful of history, and so it is no surprise that the schools use its many historical sites and museums as "extended classrooms." The school system, under the strong leadership of Superintendent Keith Rohwer, serves approximately 1,350 students, K–12. It has received high ratings in both student performance and assessment quality under STARS. But Nebraska City Public Schools is perhaps best known in the state for its comprehensive approach to what educators there call "public partnerships."

Teresa Frields, District Assessment Coordinator,
and Julie Dutton, Sixth-Grade Teacher

The Focus on Public Partnerships

Nebraska City Public Schools (NCPS) strives to provide high-quality educational opportunities for students and recognizes that learning is a lifelong process. As a district, we continually review curriculum, assessment, instruction, and learning goals to maintain a clear vision of how best to teach students. As an integral part of the process, we recognize the need to keep the community and public ties close. Teachers and students utilize these educational partners, as well as the abundant resources of the community, to enrich student learning.

Our work is guided by a clear district mission statement and statement of beliefs, at the heart of which is the expectation that *"all* students will be safe, respectful, and responsible citizens, thrive in a culturally diverse environment, learn through cooperative efforts, think and solve problems creatively, and become technologically proficient."* Although NCPS has always supported rigorous academic standards, with the advent of STARS, we have been able to use the data collected and analyzed each year to drive instructional decision making. And importantly, we have shared this information with the public, giving parents and community members regular opportunities to view how the district engages its curriculum and its balanced assessment program as ongoing processes. These opportunities include Brown Bag Series presentations, at which teachers and administrators share information informally in one-hour, lunchtime presentations and discussions at a central community location; an annual Focus on Education program that invites parents and community members into the school to learn about curriculum, instruction, and assessment; and regular school board presentations following the release of the state report cards.

We attempt to make these forums as interactive as possible. For example, while the Focus on Education program used to be merely presentational, it has evolved over time to showcase the district's assessment, curriculum, and instruction by giving parents and community members a hands-on look at teachers sharing their craft. A typical agenda for Focus on Education might look like this:

1. dinner/agenda and handouts

2. welcome from school leaders stating purpose of event

3. recognition of those in attendance

4. overview of district philosophy

5. teachers' demonstration lessons

6. story boards: visual representations of standards-based lessons and examples of assessments (in each subject at all grade levels)

The teacher demonstrations are always a hit with parents. During that portion of the evening, attendees simply choose a twenty-minute session to attend. They will pick two or three sessions so that they have a chance to be part of several different learning experiences. These demonstrations are standards based and include some discussion of the standard being taught, the district curriculum aligned to the standard, and the assessment used to measure student learning. Teachers teach the lesson, and attendees actually take the assessment. Teachers provide a visual representation of the lesson and have handouts for participants.

At a recent Focus on Education evening, Julie demonstrated the following sixth-grade lesson on effective scientific communication:

1. You will be given a simple picture [see Figure 6–2 for example]. Study it for a few minutes. Then formulate a plan as to how you will describe the picture to your partner. Where will you start? What words will you use? Remember that you cannot tell your partner what the picture is. You can only describe what you see. Take a few minutes to write a paragraph plan.

2. Next, with your partner, take turns describing the picture to each other. Give each other directions on how to draw the picture. As you listen to your partner describe the picture, attempt to draw it yourself (and then switch roles).

3. When you have both completed your drawings, compare the actual pictures and the ones you drew from your partner's description. Answer these questions:

   ◆ How well do you think you communicated what you saw?

   ◆ What process did you use to describe your picture?

   ◆ What part did you describe first? Why did you decide to start there?

   ◆ What did you leave out? Did you miscommunicate anything?

Figure 6–2 Sample Picture for Scientific Communication Exercise

♦ Finally, how could you have communicated your information more clearly?

Both students and adults enjoy this simple activity, which can be used as a building block for more complex scientific descriptions. Even at this simple level, students and adults identify insightful and detailed improvements they can make in their descriptive process. They see the need for clear communication, both written and oral, in scientific observation.

With adults, a discussion follows about how the activity fits into the state standards. Their comments after the activity say it all:

"This was really fun."

"I wish we had done science like this when I was in school."

"All we ever did in science back then was memorize facts and long lists of vocabulary. I don't remember any of it."

Each year, NCPS attempts to involve more staff in an effort to include as many educators as possible. We've also invited various guests, including state senators, the state commissioner of education, staff from the Nebraska department of education and our educational service unit, and representatives of higher education. Although we change the format of Focus on Education each year to ensure that it remains fresh and interesting, it is always a perfect venue to share with and thank our educational partners for their efforts to help our students grow and our schools improve.

Twenty-First-Century School-Community Relationships

Nebraska City's focus on public partnerships is unique to its particular circumstances, but as the Annenberg Institute's report *Reasons for Hope, Voices for Change* (1998) makes evident, it is far from an isolated example. That report catalogs no fewer that 174 "public engagement" projects from around the country, and those were only a cross-section of the total number the institute found. We might say that Annenberg's answer to Kettering was that rumors of the public's demise—and its interest in public schooling—were exaggerated.

But even in 1998, before the advent of NCLB, this irrepressibly sanguine report found that such projects are immensely difficult to sustain over time and to bring to "scale" (47–50). It also found that "teachers are not yet a significant force in public engagement" (49). Now, almost ten years and one test-based federal law later, that prospect seems dimmer than ever. Instead of invitations to conversation of the sort we see in Nebraska City, most communities get little more than the equivalent of stock reports. Educators' dealings with parents and other community members are largely about getting the numbers right.

But if we want more than what the accountability agenda offers— if we want engaging schools that foster rich *inter*action, rather than simple *trans*actions—then public engagement is not about getting the numbers right; it's about getting the relationships right (Meier 2002). Deborah Meier, longtime teacher and principal, makes it clear that this work is never simple or easy, especially in racially and linguistically diverse environments. Racism and cultural assumptions often get in the way of working effectively with all families. Sometimes, educators *will* fail families; sometimes, families will fail schools. But as Meier insists, "openness to a family's questions and concerns— even about what makes us trustworthy—is a constituent part of being a good teacher at any school" (43).

Getting the relationships right begins with teacher leadership. Building engaged school-community relationships is not a matter of giving the school over to parents or opening the door to private interests. Rather, it is about working together to support student learning and school improvement. And the surest way to do that is to support educators' capacity building. While important decisions about childrens' learning should be made collaboratively, teachers take the lead in fostering their learning in school, just as we would expect a doctor to take the lead in treating childrens' health in the office or the hospital. Administrators, parents, other community members, staff developers, policy makers and politicians—all other educational partners help teachers teach and students learn. They help ensure that teachers have the tools they need and the trust necessary to do their jobs.

As the literature on school-community partnerships makes clear, *trust* is the key word. Once again, Deborah Meier says it best: "all parents [and other community members] need ways to make informed judgments about the professional competence of the school" (2002, 53). This means doing what Nebraska City educators do: opening the doors of the school, sharing the work being done by students and teachers, being responsive to questions and concerns, and maintaining dialogue with parents and other community members. At times, it means giving those educational partners specific and formal roles in school improvement efforts or otherwise drawing on the important resources they bring to the table. But teachers must have ample opportunities to build, sustain, and demonstrate their professional expertise.

The final chapter of the Nebraska Story is not yet written, but if it were, it would tell the tale of Nebraska teachers leading the way to community-based school improvement through standards and assessment. The narrative would surely feature schools made stronger by the rich relationships they fostered with parents and other community members. In some cases, it also would feature communities made stronger, even renewed, because as Nebraskans have long known, schools and communities are symbiotic. In any event, whether or not this part of the story ever gets past draft form under STARS, it offers a hopeful glimpse of what might lie beyond the regressive accountability agenda.

Notes

1. The school depicted here is not included in the Comprehensive Evaluation Project data. Also, this rendering is a composite of more than one such event.

2. The following is excerpted from a CEP interview.

3. In fact, "impoverished public life" doesn't go nearly far enough. We are besieged by social ills. My own partial list would include terrorism, a war on terrorism, school violence, persistent poverty, environmental degradation, insufficient health care, routine violations of our civil liberties by a dangerously overreaching executive branch, the consolidation of media as well as the global food supply, corporate welfare, renewed attacks on

women's reproductive rights, widespread and socially sanctioned violence against women, human rights abuses perpetrated by our own government around the globe, gaping holes in the social safety net for our most vulnerable citizens, xenophobic immigration policies, a racially unjust penal system, the resegregation of schools, and the erosion of workers' rights—for a start! (For some startling statistics on life for many children in the United States today see www.childrensdefense.org or www.aecf.org.) If Hurricanes Katrina and Rita and the governmental response to them demonstrated anything, it's that abiding racial and class-based social dysfunction is a defining feature of life in the United States.

4. See, for example, Bracey (2004), Karp (2004), Kohn (2004a).

5. This is also a consistent finding of the Phi Delta Kappa/Gallup polls cited in Chapter 2 and of a poll conducted by the American Association of School Administrators; see Decker and Decker (2003).

6. Similarly, the Annenberg Institute identifies seven types of public engagement: parent participation, community/parent organizing, standards development/implementation, strategic planning/community visioning, public conversation and deliberation, governance/shared decision making, and legislative policy development (1998, 84–85).

7. There are a number of organizations and networks devoted to school-community partnerships; these include the Annenberg Institute for School Reform (www.annenberginstitute.org), the Coalition for Community Schools (www.communityschools.org), the Center on School, Family, and Community Partnerships (www.csos.jhu.edu/p2000/center.htm) and its National Network of Partnership Schools, the Rural School and Community Trust (http://ruraledu.org), and the National Center for Family and Community Connections with Schools (www.sedl.org/connections). Several other organizations and networks have done extensive work in this area, including Mid-continent Research for Education and Learning, the Northwest Regional Educational Laboratory (www.nwrel.org), the Southwest Educational Development Laboratory (www.sedl.org), and the Coalition of Essential Schools (www.essentialschools.org).

8. This list could go on. For a sampling of community-based student projects in Nebraska, see Brooke (2003b) and *Authentic Evaluation* (2000).

9. Indeed, as early as our first year of research, 76 percent of language arts teachers surveyed reported that their local standards and assessment process had improved communication with parents (Bandalos 2002, 55).

10. Nebraska's immigrant and refugee populations are growing rapidly. Between 1990 and 2000, according to Census 2000 data, the Latino pop-

ulation grew by 155 percent. The state is also home to many refugee families from Somalia, Vietnam, Iraq, Bosnia, and elsewhere. For more information on demographic changes in Nebraska and services and initiatives for new Nebraskans, see the websites of the Grantmakers Concerned with Immigrants and Refugees (www.gcir.org), the Nebraska Humanities Council (www.nebraskahumanities.org), and Nebraska Appleseed (www.neappleseed.org).

11. Unfortunately, as I mentioned in Chapter 3, these ties are currently being challenged by a state law requiring the dissolution of Nebraska's two hundred or so Class I, or elementary only, districts in summer 2006. It is obviously too early to ascertain what the fallout from these dissolutions will be, but in an era when the benefits of small schools are becoming clearer and clearer, this development is worrisome indeed.

12. As in other chapters, schools identified by name are not necessarily included in the Comprehensive Evaluation Project study.

Conclusion
Reclaiming the Profession

As I write these words—early morning, as day breaks—my two daughters sleep soundly upstairs. Because it's summer, and because I am looking forward to what is sure to be a wonderful but challenging day with them, I am thinking of their teachers—who, I am quite sure, also have known wonderful but challenging days with the girls. I am thinking of the trust my wife and I place in these professionals five days a week, week after week, year after year. I am thinking of how important these adults have been in the kids' lives as role models, inspirations, and conversation partners. Teachers have torn them down, and teachers have built them up. Teachers have wounded them, and teachers have given them the strength to heal. Teachers have dismissed their concerns, and teachers have listened carefully to them. Sure, the girls spend most of their lives outside of school, and hundreds of other people—starting, I hope, with their parents—shape who they are, as well. But just as surely, teachers matter in their young lives. They matter because they are relationship builders, practitioners of a delicate, adaptive art.

But thanks to the accountability agenda and its relentless assault on teachers, these people to whom we (like millions of other parents) entrust our children are treated less like professional artists than shiftless functionaries. Instead of equipping teachers with the tools and the trust they need to do their jobs well, that agenda has painted teachers as selfish, lazy, and incompetent. It has stripped them of their professionalism by handing them scripts and making them servants of remote "experts" who likely never stepped foot in a classroom and know nothing about teaching and learning. It has hijacked assessment, reduced staff development to test prep or rendered it irrelevant altogether, and sown the seeds of distrust for teachers and schools among the public. It has stolen the trust, respect, and support that practitioners of this art deserve, poisoning their relationships with educational partners. And when teachers *have* tried to assert the professionalism to which they have every right—especially in groups, and most especially in unions—the accountability agenda has been ever ready to charge "the education establishment" with the building of elitist enclaves.

This agenda has been so successful, in fact, that the federal government has passed a law that says teacher knowledge does not count. I wish this were hyperbole. As many observers have noted, the phrases "scientifically based" and "research based" appear more than one hundred times in the No Child Left Behind Act.[1] The act defines "scientifically based research" as "research that involves the application of rigorous, systematic, and objective procedures to obtain reliable and valid knowledge relevant to education activities and programs" (One Hundred Seventh United States Congress 2002, 540). Further specifications include the use of experimental or quasi-experimental design and acceptance by "independent experts." What they do not include: teacher research, teacher observation, teacher judgment.

In fact, these requirements consummate the twentieth-century positivist dream of replacing messy human judgment with scientific rigor and precision. At the end of the first decade of that century, John Dewey warned that overreaching claims to scientific certainty in education were likely to lead to a "rigid orthodoxy" and "a dead monotonous uniformity of practice" ([1910] 1964, 172).[2] Nonetheless, the rise of positivism led to an intense interest in developing a "new science of education" that would replace educators' "hunches and guesses" with exact psychometric measurements and scientifically derived "effective practices."[3] This new science, a peculiar American secular faith, was responsible for many of the "innovations" of twentieth-century schooling, including tracking, vocational education, the use of business methods of planning and budgeting in schools, the Taylorization (scientific management) of teachers' work, and of course standardized testing. Today, of course, psychometricians are major players in education, the search continues unabated for the Perfect Test, and "scientifically based research" *by law* drives educational practice.

Now, science has made important contributions to education; mine is not an antiscience argument. It *is* an argument against the notion that all teaching and learning can be reduced to precise measurement through "objective" instrumentation and that such measurement supersedes the trained observation and judgment of teaching professionals. It's not science or scientists from whom teachers and their allies must reclaim the profession; it's the accountability agenda, which in its fascination for exactitude and simplicity has fashioned a fetishized "science" that few practicing scientists or science educators whom I know would want to defend.

Teachers should, of course, use the tools of science to inform their practice; the point is that objective science itself is not the teaching instrument—the teacher is. Noted physician Eric Cassell (1997) makes a similar point about doctors. In his fascinating book *Doctoring*, he argues that twentieth-century medicine installed "impersonal objective medical science" as the "instrument of care," rather than the trained, observing physician (7). Cassell calls on his profession to reinstate the doctor and her relationship with patients to the center of primary care medicine. This doctor will use cutting-edge and proven diagnostic technology, but only as part of an overall approach to primary care that centers on clinical judgment, a capacity that relies first and foremost on *listening* to the patient (taking a history). After all, the important thing is not knowing how to run tests, but knowing when to use them, how to evaluate their results, and what to do in response to them (162). This knowledge, forged through training, experience, and collaboration with other health care professionals, derives from "practical wisdom," or what Aristotle would call *phronesis*. It can never emerge directly from the science, Cassell insists; physicians "are the means, the relationship with the patient is the vehicle, and the clinical method the tool by which this knowledge is gained" (125).

My claim here parallels Cassell's. To paraphrase him: Teachers are the means, the relationship with students is the vehicle, and professional judgment is the tool by which teachers gain practical wisdom. This claim is similar to those offered in defense of what is generally referred to as teachers' "craft knowledge" (Barth 2001; Burney 2004).[4] But craft knowledge may not go far enough. It's not just that teachers know things because they have experience in classrooms; it's that they develop a deep understanding of (or wisdom about) how to bring that knowledge to bear in irreducibly complex situations as part of their adaptive, relational art: their art of engagement.

The previous three chapters were devoted to what we might think of as *forms of engagement*, each emerging from relations of mutual responsibility with educational partners and each shaped by the shared goals of student learning and school improvement. The first and most fundamental form of engagement is *pedagogical*: the relationship between teachers and students. The primary aim is to connect students to their own learning—to lure them, as it were, into active involvement in their own education. The second form of engagement is *collegial*: the relationship between teachers and other educators. The primary aim here is to connect colleagues to a collaborative school improvement effort. The third form of engagement is *communal*: the relationship between teachers and the larger community. The primary aim here is to connect parents and other community members to that same collaborative effort.

Of course, I am teasing out only a few threads of an extraordinarily complex web of relationships and responsibilities. And I am focusing only on teachers' responsibilities, though I've insisted throughout this book that these relationships must be reciprocal; each responsibility on the part of a teacher triggers corresponding responsibilities for other educational partners. Nonetheless, these are the rudiments of what we might think of as *engaged professionalism*.

This notion—engaged professionalism—is important because it allows teachers to reclaim their profession without falling into cleverly placed verbal traps that associate *any* assertion of professionalism as what George Bernard Shaw called "conspiracies against the laity" (1913, xxii). This latter, traditional notion holds that professions are insulated and insular, constituted by specialized, often jealously guarded bodies of knowledge, skills, discourses, and standards for practice. But this understanding of professions is historically specific and in fact anachronistic (Gallagher 2005). It was a product of the late nineteenth and early twentieth centuries, when frightening social change, economic shifts and expansion, the rise of positivist science, and a wholesale bureaucratization of U.S. society conspired to produce a whole new class of management experts, including in education. In many ways, these experts *did* perpetrate a conspiracy against the laity: they put control of social institutions, including public ones, into very few hands. It is this model of professionalism that critics have in mind when they assail teachers for "asserting their professional prerogatives" and "hiding behind eduspeak."

But while managerial professionalism is very much with us today,[5] it's neither the only option nor the one that most teachers actually practice. (Though it *is* the one practiced by those experts who would control teachers' work from afar.) Engaging teachers view relationship building with educational partners inside and outside of schools as a professional responsibility. In the name of democratic dialogue, engaging teachers use their expertise to *expand*, rather than constrict, access to public conversations. Their knowledge, their expertise, counts; they know things about teaching and learning that others do not. However, their job is not to guard this expertise, but to share it, starting with sponsoring reflective deliberation about the nature and purpose of teaching and learning among all their educational partners. In this way, engaging teachers both claim their expertise and share it, thereby deepening and extending it. They become, in short, community organizers.

Perhaps all this sounds like a tall order; don't teachers have enough to do in the classroom? Well, it *is* a tall order. As we've seen in Nebraska, teacher leadership is a great deal of work. But the Nebraska Story also teaches us that when teachers experience engaged professionalism for themselves, and when they see the results for their students, they find themselves and their schools invigorated. They also find that many allies (or, at least, potential allies) are waiting for them on the other side of that classroom door.

Besides, as Cathy Fleischer points out, teachers are *by definition* community organizers: people who design structures and forums that involve people in collective reflection, decision making, and self-governance (2000, 77).[6] Good teachers have always done this in their classrooms. Teacher-leaders extend this work into schools and larger communities as well. They "come out of private practice" to mobilize various educational partners to "pull in the same direction," as Nebraska educators would say.[7]

It is time for teachers and students, along with their allies, to take teaching and learning back. In fact, as the rise of coalitions against NCLB and high-stakes testing around the country suggests, the struggle has already begun.[8] The groundswell of criticism and activism in response to NCLB and high-stakes testing continues to grow; teachers, students, parents, other community members, state legislators and policymakers, and organizations and unions are finding opportunities to work together for change. And as this happens, more and more people are learning to respect and value the hard work of teaching and learning.

In my hopeful moments, I believe this groundswell of grassroots activism means the educational agenda for the twenty-first century is being rewritten. This emerging agenda calls for policies, processes, and practices that are

◆ teacher led, not teacher fed

◆ school and community based, not standardized

◆ supportive, not punitive

◆ learning focused, not achievement obsessed

◆ equitable, not rationed by race or class

◆ based on rich interactions, not bottom-line transactions

◆ diversity rich, not one-size-fits-all

◆ commitment oriented, not compliance oriented

◆ founded on earned trust, not unearned distrust

◆ inclusive of all kids and teachers, not only those who produce high scores

Of course, this is just a start. But if we really want to leave no child behind, this agenda—the engagement agenda—has a far better chance of moving beyond otherwise empty slogans than does the disastrous accountability agenda.

My fondest wish—call it a prayer—for this book is that the Nebraska Story serves as a tool to think with and source of hope for this reclamation project. Obviously, what has happened in this unique and in some ways strange state cannot be replicated elsewhere; in fact, one of the lessons of this story is that quality education emerges from and is responsive to its specific context. Nor is the Nebraska Story an unalloyed tale of progress and accomplishment; the state and its districts and schools have made mistakes, and they have a great deal of work to do to achieve their goals. But at its best, the story shows what becomes possible when teachers are at the lead and schools are in the center of school improvement.

And that's what stories are for; they lay bare what Adrienne Rich (2002) calls "the arts of the possible." So whatever happens to STARS, or to NCLB for that matter, I am hopeful that we—those of us who care about the fate of public education in our diverse democracy—will build on this story, rewrite it, and perhaps write a new one altogether. Here's hoping this new story and the new world we create with it are deserving of our children and of the noble, professional art of teaching.

Notes

1. Burney (2004, 526); my search for the combined phrase "scientifically based research" revealed seventeen uses in the executive summary alone and sixty-nine uses in the body of the act.

2. Dewey believed science is best understood as "a system of possible predicates—that is, of possible standpoints or methods to be employed

in qualifying some particular experience whose nature is not clear to us" ([1903] 1964, 33). Like many scientists and science educators today, Dewey viewed science not as a static body of knowledge, but rather as a method of inquiry and the always provisional knowledge produced by that method.

3. See Lynne (2004), Gallagher (2002b), Tyack and Cuban (1995), Spring (1990), Cremin (1961), Callahan (1962), and Sacks (1999).

4. Barth defines craft knowledge as "the massive collection of experiences and learning that those who live and work under the roof of the schoolhouse inevitably accrue during their careers" (2001, 83). Burney claims that teachers, "like doctors, already possess a great deal of craft knowledge—a mixture of expertise, theories, propositions, and tacit knowledge applied in the daily conduct of their practice" and wishes to see it "codified, tested, and shared" (2004, 527).

5. In fact, Michael Apple convincingly traces what he calls "new managerialism," in which "a relatively autonomous fraction of the managerial and professional class has taken on even more power in directing social and educational policies" (2001, 29).

6. Fleischer's book centers on working collaboratively with parents. She offers both useful, concrete advice and a sturdy rationale for thinking of community engagement as part of the work of teaching.

7. This understanding of teacher leadership is informed by the literature that has grown around this topic over the past twenty years, beginning with the Holmes Group (1986) and Carnegie Task Force on Teaching as a Profession (1986) reports and taking shape in work by Wasley (1991), Barth (2001), Westheimer (1998), Wolfe and Antinarella (1997), Lieberman and Miller (2004), and others.

8. A wealth of information on these coalitions is available on the FairTest website (www.fairtest.org), including state-by-state resources and contacts, links to position statements about high-stakes testing by a variety of organizations and unions, accessible fact sheets and papers, an organizational toolkit, a media guide, policy resources, and so on. The site includes information for teachers, parents, students, and concerned citizens and is an excellent place to start for anyone who wishes to get involved in the struggle against high-stakes testing and NCLB.

References

Amrein, Audrey, and David Berliner. 2003. "The Effects of High-Stakes Testing on Student Motivation and Learning." *Educational Leadership* 60 (February): 32–37.

Annenberg Institute. 1998. *Reasons for Hope, Voices for Change*. Report. Accessed at www.annenberginstitute.org/images/Reasons.pdf.

Apple, Michael W. 1993. *Official Knowledge*. New York: Routledge.

———. 2001. *Educating the "Right" Way*. New York: Routledge.

Authentic Evaluation: Nebraska Teachers Design Assessment Through Active Classroom Learning. 2000. Handbook. Lincoln, NE: Goals 2000 Assessment Project.

Bambino, Deborah. 2002. "Critical Friends." *Educational Leadership* 59 (March): 25–27.

Bandalos, Deborah. 2002. "Language Arts Assessment." In *Charting STARS: The State of Assessment in the State of Nebraska* (report), by Chris Gallagher. Lincoln, NE. Available at www.nde.state.ne.us/stars/documents/yearonereport.all.pdf.

———. 2003. "Evaluation of District Language Arts Assessments." In *Charting STARS: Sustainability as Challenge and Opportunity* (report) by Chris Gallagher. Lincoln, NE. Available at www.nde.state.ne.us/stars/pdf/year2stars.pdf.

Barth, Roland S. 2001. *Learning by Heart*. San Francisco: Jossey-Bass.

Beadie, Nancy. 2004. "Moral Errors and Strategic Mistakes: Lessons from the History of Student Accountability." In *Holding Accountability Accountable: What Ought to Matter in Public Education*, ed. Kenneth A. Sirotnik. New York: Teachers College Press.

Benton, Joshua, and Holly K. Hacker. 2004. "Poor Schools' TAKS Surges Raise Cheating Questions." DallasNews.com, December 19. Accessed at www.dallasnews.com/sharedcontent/dws/news/longterm/stories/121904dnmetcheating.64fa3.html.

Berliner, David, and Bruce Biddle. 1995. *The Manufactured Crisis*. Reading, MA: Addison-Wesley.

Berry, Barnet, Mandy Hoke, and Eric Hirsch. 2004. "The Search for Highly Qualified Teachers." *Phi Delta Kappan* 85 (May): 684–89.

Black, Paul, Christine Harrison, Clare Lee, Bethan Marshall, and Dylan Wiliam. 2004. "Working Inside the Black Box: Assessment for Learning in the Classroom." *Phi Delta Kappan* 86 (September): 8–21.

Black, Paul, and Dylan Wiliam. 1998. "Inside the Black Box: Raising Standards through Classroom Assessment." *Phi Delta Kappan* 80 (October): 139–48.

Bracey, Gerald. 2002. *The War Against America's Public Schools.* Boston: Allyn and Bacon.

———. 2003. "April Foolishness: The 20th Anniversary of *A Nation at Risk.*" *Phi Delta Kappan* 84 (April): 621.

———. 2004. "The Perfect Law." *Dissent* (42). Accessed at www.dissentmagazine.org/article/?article=318.

Broad, Bob. 2003. *What We Really Value.* Logan: Utah State University Press.

Brooke, Robert E. 2003a. "Introduction: Place-Conscious Education, Rural Schools, and the Nebraska Writing Project's Rural Voices, Country Schools Team." In *Rural Voices: Place-Conscious Education and the Teaching of Writing,* ed. Robert E. Brooke. New York: Teachers College Press/National Writing Project.

———. 2003b. *Rural Voices: Place-Conscious Education and the Teaching of Writing.* New York: Teachers College Press/National Writing Project.

Brookhart, Susan M. 2003. "Developing Measurement Theory for Classroom Assessment: Purposes and Uses." *Educational Measurement: Issues and Practice* 22 (December): 5–12.

———. 2005. "The Quality of Local District Assessments Used in Nebraska's School-Based, Teacher-Led Assessment and Reporting System." *Educational Measurement: Issues and Practice* 24 (June): 12–21.

Buckendahl, Chad, Barbara Plake, and James Impara. 2004. "A Strategy for Evaluating District Developed Assessment for State Accountability." *Educational Measurement: Issues and Practice* 23 (June): 17–25.

Burney, Deanna. 2004. "Craft Knowledge: The Road to Transforming Schools." *Phi Delta Kappan* 85 (March): 526–31.

Callahan, Raymond. 1962. *Education and the Cult of Efficiency.* Chicago: University of Chicago Press.

Capers, Melissa. 2004. "Epilogue: Teaching and Shared Professional Practice—A History of Resistance; A Future Dependent on Its Embrace." In *Learning Together, Leading Together: Changing Schools Through Professional Learning Communities,* ed. Shirley M. Hord. New York: Teachers College Press.

Carnegie Task Force on Teaching as a Profession. 1986. *A Nation Prepared: Teachers for the 21st Century.* New York: Carnegie Foundation.

Cassell, Eric J. 1997. *Doctoring: The Nature of Primary Care Medicine.* New York: Oxford University Press.

Center for Rural Affairs Committee on Education. 2000. "A School at the Center: Community-Based Education and Rural Redevelopment." Lincoln, NE: School at the Center.

Chadwick, Kathy Gardner. 2004. *Improving Schools Through Community Engagement: A Practical Guide for Educators.* Thousand Oaks, CA: Corwin.

Christensen, Douglas. 2001a. "Building State Assessment from the Classroom Up." *School Administrator* Web edition, December. Accessed at www.aasa.org/publications/saarticledetail.cfm?Item Number=2746&snItemNumber=950&tnItemNumber=951.

———. 2001b. Press Conference Remarks. Lincoln, NE, November 9.

———. 2004. "Accountability in Nebraska." *Education Gadfly* May 13. Accessed at www.edexcellence.net/foundation/gadfly/index.cfm.

Clinchy, Evans. 2004. "Reimagining Public Education." *Phi Delta Kappan* 85 (February): 448–50.

Cochran-Smith, Marilyn, and Susan L. Lytle. 1993. *Inside/Outside.* New York: Teachers College Press.

Commission on Excellence in Education. 1983. *A Nation at Risk.* Report. Accessed at www.ed.gov/pubs/NatAtRisk/risk.html.

Copperman, Paul. 1978. *The Literacy Hoax: The Decline of Reading, Writing, and Learning in the Public Schools and What We Can Do About It.* New York: Morrow.

Corbett, Dick. 2000. "Reaching All Students: The Real Challenge of Reform." In *Accountability, Assessment, and Teacher Commitment: Lessons from Kentucky's Reform Efforts,* ed. Betty Lou White and Kevin Jones. Albany: State University of New York Press.

Cremin, Lawrence. 1961. *The Transformation of the School.* New York: Vintage.

Cronbach, Lee J. 1990. *Essentials of Psychological Testing.* 5th ed. New York: Harper.

Cunningham, William G. 2003. "Grassroots Democracy: Putting the Public Back into Public Education." *Phi Delta Kappan* 84 (June): 776–79.

Darling-Hammond, Linda. 1997. *The Right to Learn.* San Francisco: Jossey-Bass.

Darling-Hammond, Linda, and Gary Sykes. 1999. *Teaching as the Learning Profession: Handbook of Policy and Practice*. San Francisco: Jossey-Bass.

Deal, Terrence, and Kent D. Peterson. 1999. *Shaping School Culture: The Heart of Leadership*. San Francisco: Jossey-Bass.

Decker, Larry E., and Virginia A. Decker. 2003. *Home, School, and Community Partnerships*. Lanham, MD: Scarecrow.

Dell'Angela, Tracy. 2004. "Nebraska Shuns State Tests." *Chicago Tribune*, April 5.1.

Dewey, John. [1900] 1956. *The School and Society*. Chicago: University of Chicago Press.

———. [1903] 1964. "Logical Conditions of a Scientific Treatment of Morality." In *John Dewey on Education*, ed. Reginald D. Archambault. Chicago: University of Chicago Press.

———. [1910] 1964. "Science as Subject-Matter and as Method." In *John Dewey on Education*, ed. Reginald D. Archambault. Chicago: University of Chicago Press.

Dobbs, Michael. 2003. "Education 'Miracle' Has a Math Problem." *Washingtonpost.com*. November 8, A.01. Accessed at www.washingtonpost.com.

Dodd, Anne Wescott, and Jean L. Konzal. 2002. *How Communities Build Stronger Schools: Stories, Strategies, and Promising Practices for Educating Every Child*. New York: Palgrave Macmillan.

Editorial Projects in Education. 1999–2005. *Quality Counts 1999, 2000, 2001, 2002, 2003, 2004, 2005*. Accessed at www.edweek.ort/re/articles/2004/10/15/qc-archives.html.

Elmore, Richard. 2004. *School Reform from the Inside Out*. Cambridge, MA: Harvard University Press.

Emery, Cathy, and Susan Ohanian. 2004. *Why Is Corporate America Bashing Our Public Schools?* Portsmouth, NH: Heinemann.

England, Crystal. 2003. *None of Our Business: Why Business Models Don't Work in Schools*. Portsmouth, NH: Heinemann.

Epstein, Joyce L., Lucretia Coates, Karen Clark Salinas, Mavis G. Sanders, and Beth S. Simon. 1997. *Schools, Family, and Community Partnerships: Your Handbook for Action*. Thousand Oaks, CA: Corwin.

Feller, Ben. 2006. "No States Meet Quality Teacher Goal" (AP). www.boston.com/news/nation/articles/2006/05/13/no_states_meet_teacher_quality_goal_set_in_federal_law/.

Fernandez, Clea, and Sonal Chokshi. 2002. "A Practical Guide to Translating Lesson Study for a U.S. Setting." *Phi Delta Kappan* 84 (October): 128–34.

Finn, Chester. 2004. "Mo' Money, Less Accountability." *Education Gadfly.* April 15. Accessed at www.edexcellence.net/institute/gadfly/issue.cfm?id=144&edition=#1771.

Fleischer, Cathy. 2000. *Teachers Organizing for Change.* Urbana, IL: National Council of Teachers of English.

Flesch, Rudolf. 1955. *Why Johnny Can't Read—and What You Can Do About It.* New York: Harper and Row.

———. 1981. *Why Johnny Still Can't Read: A New Look at the Scandal of Our Schools.* New York: Harper and Row.

Foster, Jack D. 2000. "A New Vision for Public Schooling." In *All Children Can Learn,* ed. Roger S. Pankratz and Joseph M. Petrosko. San Francisco: Jossey-Bass.

Fullan, Michael. 1993. *Change Forces: Probing the Depths of Educational Reform.* New York: Falmer.

———. 2001. *Leading in a Culture of Change.* San Francisco: Jossey-Bass.

Funk, Patricia E., and Jon M. Bailey. 2000. *Trampled Dreams: The Neglected Economy of the Rural Plains.* Walthill, NE: Center for Rural Affairs. Accessed at www.cfa.org/pdf/Trampled_Dreams.pdf.

Gallagher, Chris W. 2000. "A Seat at the Table." *Phi Delta Kappan* 81 (March): 502–7.

———. 2002a. *Charting STARS: The State of Assessment in the State of Nebraska.* Report. Lincoln, NE. Available at www.nde.state.ne.us/stars/documents/yearonereport.all.pdf.

———. 2002b. *Radical Departures: Composition and Progressive Pedagogy.* Urbana, IL: National Council of Teachers of English.

———. 2003. *Charting STARS: Sustainability as Challenge and Opportunity.* Report. Lincoln, NE. Available at www.nde.state.ne.us/stars/pdf/year2stars.pdf.

———. 2004a. *Charting STARS: New Conversations.* Report. Lincoln, NE. Available at www.nde.state.ne.us/stars/documents/chartingstars.y3.pdf.

———. 2004b. "Turning the Accountability Tables." *Phi Delta Kappan* 85 (January): 352–60.

———. 2005. "We Compositionists: Toward Engaged Professionalism." *JAC* 25 (1): 75–99.

Gerstner, Lou V. Jr., Roger D. Semerad, Denis P. Doyle, and William B. Johnston. 1994. *Reinventing Education.* New York: Dutton.

Goldberg, Mark. 2005. "Test Mess 2." *Phi Delta Kappan* 86 (January): 390–91.

Goldenberg, Claude. 2004. *Successful School Change*. New York: Teachers College Press.

Goldhaber, Dan, and Jane Hannaway. 2004. "Accountability with a Kicker." *Phi Delta Kappan* 85 (April): 598–605.

Gray, James. 1986. "University of California, Berkeley: The Bay Area Writing Project and the National Writing Project." In *School-College Collaborative Programs in English*, ed. Ron Fortune. New York: Modern Language Association.

Guskey, Thomas. 2003. "How Classroom Assessments Improve Learning." *Educational Leadership* 60 (February): 6–11.

Hamburger, Tom, and Peter Wallsten. 2005. "Inquiry Finds White House Role in Contract." *Los Angeles Times*, April 16, A14.

Haney, Walter, George Madaus, and Robert Lyons. 1993. *The Fractured Marketplace for Standardized Testing*. Boston: Kluwer Academic.

Hargreaves, Andy. 1995. *Changing Teachers, Changing Times*. Toronto: Ontario Institute for Studies in Education.

Hargreaves, Andy, Lorna Earl, Shawn Moore, and Susan Manning. 2001. *Learning to Change*. San Francisco: Jossey-Bass.

Hawley, Willis D., and Linda Vallie. 1999. "The Essentials of Effective Professional Development: A New Consensus." In *Teaching as the Learning Profession: Handbook of Policy and Practice*, eds. Linda Darling-Hammond and Gary Sykes. San Francisco: Jossey-Bass.

Henning-Stout, Mary. 1994. *Responsive Assessment*. San Francisco: Jossey-Bass.

Hillocks, George. 2002. *The Testing Trap: How State Writing Assessments Control Learning*. New York: Teachers College Press.

Hirsch, E. D. 1988. *Cultural Literacy: What Every American Needs to Know*. New York: Vintage.

Holmes Group. 1986. *Tomorrow's Teachers*. East Lansing, MI: Holmes Group.

Hord, Shirley M., ed. 2004. *Learning Together, Leading Together: Changing Schools Through Professional Learning Communities*. New York: Teachers College Press.

"Houston Schools to Fire Six Teachers in Cheating Scandal." 2005. *CNN.com.*, May 5. Accessed at www.cnn.com/2005/education/as/as/houstonschools.ap/index.html.

Huffman, Jane B., and Kristine K. Hipp. 2003. *Reculturing Schools as Professional Learning Communities*. Lanham, MD: Scarecrow.

Hunt, Thomas C. 2005. "Education Reforms: Lessons from History." *Phi Delta Kappan* 87 (September): 84–89.

Huot, Brian. 2002. *(Re)Articulating Writing Assessment for Teaching and Learning.* Logan: Utah State University Press.

Isernhagen, Jody. 2005. *Charting STARS: Voice from the Field.* Report. Lincoln, NE. Available at www.nde.state.ne.us/stars/documents/ yearfourfinalreportbysusan9-16-05.pdf.

Joel, Steve. 2001. "Off the Bandwagon in Nebraska: A Local View." *School Administrator* Web edition, December. Accessed at www.aasa.org/publications/content.cfm?itemnumber=2747.

Johnston, Peter H. 1992. *Constructive Evaluation of Literate Activity.* New York: Longman.

Karp, Stan. 2004. "NCLB's Selective Vision of Equality: Some Gaps Count More than Others." In *Many Children Left Behind,* ed. Deborah Meier and George Wood. Boston: Beacon.

Kohn, Alfie. 1999. *The Schools Our Children Deserve.* New York: Houghton-Mifflin.

———. 2000. *The Case Against Standardized Testing.* Portsmouth, NH: Heinemann.

———. 2004a. "NCLB and the Effort to Privatize Education." In *Many Children Left Behind,* ed. Deborah Meier and George Wood. Boston: Beacon.

———. 2004b. "Test Today, Privatize Tomorrow." *Phi Delta Kappan* 85 (April): 569–77.

Kozol, Jonathan. 2005. *The Shame of the Nation: The Restoration of Apartheid Schooling in America.* New York: Crown.

Langer, Judith A. 2004. *Getting to Excellent.* New York: Teachers College Press.

Lefkowits, Laura, and Kirsten Miller. 2006. "Fulfilling the Promise of the Standards Movement." *Phi Delta Kappan* 87 (January): 403–7.

Lessinger, Leon. 1970. *Every Kid a Winner: Accountability in Schooling.* New York: Simon and Schuster.

Lieberman, Ann, and Laura Miller. 2004. *Teacher Leadership.* San Francisco: Jossey-Bass.

Lieberman, Ann, and Diane R. Wood. 2003. *Inside the National Writing Project.* New York: Teachers College Press.

Linn, Robert L. 2000. "Assessments and Accountability." *Educational Researcher* 29 (March): 4–16.

Lukin, Leslie E., Deborah L. Bandalos, Teresa J. Eckhout, and Kristine Mickelson. 2004. "Facilitating the Development of Assessment Literacy." *Educational Measurement: Issues and Practice* 23 (June): 26–32.

Lyn, Darren. 2005. "HISD Fires Two Teachers Over TAKS Test Cheating Scandal." *ABC13.com.*, February 17. Accessed at www.khou.com/topstories/stories/khou050217_jt_hisd.ba1200c9.html.

Lynne, Patricia. 2004. *Coming to Terms: A Theory of Writing Assessment.* Logan: Utah State University Press.

MacDaniels, Carol, with Robert E. Brooke. 2003. "Developing School/Community Connections: The Nebraska Writing Project's Rural Institute Program." In *Rural Voices: Place-Conscious Education and the Teaching of Writing,* ed. Robert E. Brooke. New York: Teachers College Press/National Writing Project.

Maclean, Norman. 1992. *A River Runs Through It and Other Stories.* New York: Simon and Schuster.

Marshak, David. 2003. "No Child Left Behind: A Foolish Race to the Past." *Phi Delta Kappan* 85 (November): 229–31.

Marshall, Margaret. 2004. *Response to Reform: Composition and the Professionalization of Teaching.* Carbondale: Southern Illinois University Press.

Mathews, David. 1996. *Is There a Public for Public Schools?* Dayton, OH: Kettering Foundation Press.

McDonald, Joseph P. 2002. "Teachers Studying Student Work: Why and How?" *Phi Delta Kappan* 84 (October): 120–27.

McLaughlin, Milbrey W., and Ida Oberman. 1996. *Teacher Learning: New Policies, New Practices.* New York: Teachers College Press.

McLaughlin, Milbrey W., and Joan E. Talbert. 2001. *Professional Communities and the Work of High School Teaching.* Chicago: University of Chicago Press.

McNeil, Linda. 2000. *Contradictions of Reform: The Educational Costs of Standardized Testing.* New York: Routledge.

Meier, Deborah. 2002. *In Schools We Trust.* Boston: Beacon.

———. 2004. "NCLB and Democracy." In *Many Children Left Behind,* eds. Deborah Meier and George Wood. Boston: Beacon.

Menand, Louis. 2001. *The Metaphysical Club: A Story of Ideas in America.* New York: Farrar, Straus, and Giroux.

Messick, Samuel. 1989. "Validity." In *Educational Measurement,* ed. Robert Linn. Washington, DC: National Council on Measurement in Education.

Meyer, Richard J., Linda Brown, Elizabeth DeNino, Kimberly Larson, Mona McKenzie, Kimberly Ridder, and Kimberly Zetterman. 1998. *Composing a Teacher Study Group.* Mahwah, NJ: Lawrence Erlbaum.

Mohr, Marian M., Courtney Rogers, Betsy Sanford, Mary Ann Nocerino, Marion S. MacLean, and Sheila Clawson. 2004. *Teacher Research for Better Schools.* New York: Teachers College Press/ National Writing Project.

Montgomery, Edward C. 2004. "What My Students Need to Know." *Letters to the Next President,* ed. Carl Glickman. New York: Teachers College Press.

Moss, Pamela A. 1992. "Shifting Conceptions of Validity in Educational Measurement: Implications for Performance Assessment." *Review of Educational Research* 62 (Autumn): 229–58.

Myatt, Larry, and Peggy Kemp. 2004. "Taking Stock: A Decade of Education Reform in Massachusetts." *Phi Delta Kappan* 86 (October): 139–44.

Neill, Monty. 2003. "Leaving Children Behind." *Phi Delta Kappan* 85 (November): 225–28.

Neill, Monty, Lisa Guisbond, and Bob Schaeffer with James Madden and Life Legeros. 2004. *Failing Our Children.* Cambridge, MA: FairTest.

Noguera, Pedro. 2004. "Standards for What? Accountability for Whom? Rethinking Standards-Based Reform in Education." In *Holding Accountability Accountable:What Ought to Matter in Public Education,* ed. Kenneth Sirotnik. New York: Teachers College Press.

Nordby, Barbara. 2005. "Top State Ed Official Disagrees With Bush." *Lincon Journal Star.* January 13. 1A.

Nye, Russell B. 1951. *Midwestern Progressive Politics.* East Lansing, MI: State College Press.

Ohanian, Susan. 2000. *One Size Fits Few: The Folly of Educational Standards.* Portsmouth, NH: Heinemann.

———. 2003. "Capitalism, Calculus, and Conscience." *Phi Delta Kappan* 84 (June): 736–47.

One Hundred Seventh United States Congress. 2002. *No Child Left Behind Act.* Reauthorization of Elementary and Secondary Education Act. HR 1/PL 107–110.

Pankake, Anita. 2004. "The Superintendent's Influence on the Creation of a Professional Learning Community." In *Learning Together, Leading Together: Changing Schools Through Professional Learning Communities,* ed. Shirley M. Hord. New York: Teachers College Press.

Pipher, Mary. 2002. *The Middle of Everywhere*. New York: Harcourt.

Plake, Barbara, James Impara, and Chad Buckendahl. 2004. "Technical Quality Criteria for Evaluating District Assessment Portfolios Used in the Nebraska STARS." *Educational Measurement: Issues and Practice* 23 (June): 12–16.

Porter-Magee, Kathleen. 2004. "Shuck Corn, Not Standards." *Education Gadfly*, May 27. Accessed at www.edexcellence.net/institute/gadfly/issue.cfm?edition=&id=150#1836.

Posner, Dave. 2004. "What's Wrong with Teaching to the Test?" *Phi Delta Kappan* 85 (June): 745–48.

Pyle, Emily. 2005. "Te$t Market." *The Texas Observer*, May 13. Accessed at www.texasobserver.org/article.php?aid=1947.

Ravitch, Diane. 1983. *The Troubled Crusade: American Education 1945–1980*. New York: Basic.

———. 2000. *Left Back: A Century of Failed School Reform*. New York: Simon and Schuster.

Reeves, Douglas B. 2002. *Holistic Accountability: Serving Students, Schools, and Community*. Thousand Oaks, CA: Corwin.

Resnick, Lauren B., and Megan Williams Hall. 1998. "Learning Organizations for Sustainable Reform." *Daedalus* 127 (Fall): 89–118.

Reville, S. Paul. 2004. "High Standards + High Stakes = High Achievement in Massachusetts." *Phi Delta Kappan* 85 (April): 591–97.

Rich, Adrienne. 2002. *The Arts of the Possible*. New York: Norton.

Robb, Laura. 2000. *Redefining Staff Development*. Portsmouth, NH: Heinemann.

Roschewski, Pat. 2003. "Nebraska STARS Line Up." *Phi Delta Kappan* 84 (March): 517–24.

———. 2004. "History and Background of Nebraska's School-Based Teacher-Led Assessment and Reporting System (STARS)." *Educational Measurement: Issues and Practice* 23 (June): 9–11.

Roschewski, Pat, with Chris Gallagher and Jody Isernhagen. 2001. "Nebraskans Reach for the STARS." *Phi Delta Kappan* 82 (April): 611–15.

Rose, Lowell, and Alec Gallup. 2002. "The 34th Annual Phi Delta Kappa/Gallup Poll of the Public's Attitudes Toward the Public Schools." *Phi Delta Kappan* 84 (September): 41–46.

———. 2003. "The 35th Annual Phi Delta Kappa/Gallup Poll of the Public's Attitudes Toward the Public Schools." *Phi Delta Kappan* 85 (September): 41–52.

———. 2004. "The 36th Annual Phi Delta Kappa/Gallup Poll of the Public's Attitudes Toward Public Schools." *Phi Delta Kappan* 86 (September): 41–52.

Sacks, Peter. 1999. *Standardized Minds*. Cambridge, MA: Perseus.

Sadker, David, and Karen Zittleman. 2004. "Test Anxiety: Are Students Failing Tests—or Are Tests Failing Students?" *Phi Delta Kappan* 85 (June): 740–44.

Sanders, Mavis G. 2006. *Building School-Community Partnerships: Collaboration for Student Success*. Thousand Oaks, CA: Corwin.

Sergiovanni, Thomas J. 1994. *Building Community in Schools*. San Francisco: Jossey-Bass.

Shaw, George Bernard. 1913. *The Doctor's Dilemma*. London: Constable and Co., Ltd.

Shor, Ira. 1986. *Culture Wars: School and Society in the Conservative Restoration, 1969–1984*. Boston: Routledge and Kegan Paul.

Sowell, Thomas. 2003. "School Performances: Part III." *Townhall.com*, September 26. Accessed at www.townhall.com/columnists/ThomasSowell/2003/09/26/school_performances_part_iii.

Spring, Joel. 1990. *The American School: 1642–1990*. 2d ed. New York: Longman.

Stiggins, Richard J. 2004a. "New Assessment Beliefs for a New School Mission." *Phi Delta Kappan* 86 (September): 22–27.

———. 2004b. *Student-Involved Classroom Assessment FOR Learning*. 4th ed. Upper Saddle River, NJ: Prentice-Hall.

———. 2005. "From Formative Assessment to Assessment FOR Learning: A Path to Success in Standards-Based Schools." *Phi Delta Kappan* 87. Available at www.pdkintl.org/kappan/k_v87/k0512sti.htm.

"Syndicator Drops Writer in Controversy." (AP). 2005. *Lincoln Journal Star*, January 9, 3A.

Theobald, Paul. 1997. *Teaching the Commons*. Boulder, CO: Westview.

Tyack, David. 1974. *One Best System: A History of American Urban Education*. Cambridge, MA: Harvard University Press.

Tyack, David, and Larry Cuban. 1995. *Tinkering Toward Utopia*. Cambridge, MA: Harvard University Press.

Wasley, Patricia. 1991. *Teachers Who Lead*. New York: Teachers College Press.

Watanabe, Tad. 2002. "Learning from Japanese Lesson Study." *Educational Leadership* 59 (March): 36–39.

Weinbaum, Alexandra, David Allen, Tina Blythe, Katherine Simon, Steve Seidel, and Catherine Rubin. 2004. *Teaching as Inquiry*. New York: Teachers College Press.

Westheimer, Joel. 1998. *Among Schoolteachers*. New York: Teachers College Press.

Wheelock, Anne. 2003. "Myopia in Massachusetts." *Educational Leadership* 61 (November): 50–54.

Will, George. 2005. "Information, Please, Not Flackery." *Lincoln Journal Star*, January 13, 5B.

Wilson, Maja. 2006. *Rethinking Rubrics in Writing Assessment*. Portsmouth, NH: Heinemann.

Wolfe, Denny, and Joseph Antinarella. 1997. *Deciding to Lead*. Portsmouth, NH: Boynton/Cook.

Wood, George. 2004. "A View from the Field: NCLB's Effects on Classrooms and Schools." In *Many Children Left Behind*, eds. Deborah Meier and George Wood. Boston: Beacon.

Index